Make Your Money Smile

Make Your Money Smile

A Personal Finance How-To-Guide to Manage, Earn, Grow, Borrow, and Protect Your Wealth

5 Pillars to Your Best Financial Life

Jason Vitug

WILEY

Published by John Wiley & Sons, Inc., Hoboken, New Jersey.
Published simultaneously in Canada.

For general information on our other products and services or for technical support,
please contact our Customer Care Department within the United States at
(800) 762-2974, outside the United States at (317) 572-3993 or fax (317) 572-4002.

Wiley also publishes its books in a variety of electronic formats. Some content that
appears in print may not be available in electronic formats. For more information
about Wiley products, visit our web site at www.wiley.com.

Library of Congress Cataloging-in-Publication Data is available:

ISBN 9781394259090(Cloth)
ISBN 9781394259137(ePDF)
ISBN 9781394259144(ePub)

Cover Design: Wiley
Design Concept: Jason Vitug

SKY10070173_032124

To all the people I've met along the way and the readers I have yet to meet, this book is dedicated to you and your well-being. Keep moving forward on the path—you're almost there!

Contents

Preface

Through the years, I've been asked about my take on the how-tos of money. I have written many step-by-step personal finance articles on dozens of websites, including my own on thesmilemoney.com. However, I never really considered writing a book on it. I know that people enjoy reading books because there's a beginning and an end, unlike online articles, where there seems to be an endless amount of information to read.

Did I really need to write this book?

You see, there are many really good how-to money books already published. I've recommended many, from Erin Lowry's *Broke Millennial* to *Get Good with Money*, written by my good friend Tiffany Aliche. They complement the mindset and habit-focused books I've written. So I initially didn't feel the need to redo what's been done quite well.

It wasn't until I had multiple conversations with people during my happiness tour that I changed my mind. One particular statement struck me profoundly: "We haven't read the how-to of money in *your* words." Indeed, some people resonate with my voice and relate to my lived experiences.

Perhaps you're one of them, and sharing my how-tos will help you reach your goals and dreams sooner. I wrote this book with a purposeful intent: to take you from where you are today to where you want to be tomorrow, and then guide you to where to go next.

This book covers the financial fundamentals and money steps aligned with my life philosophies. *Make Your Money Smile* is the third book of the financial wellness series. It follows *You Only Live Once* (a book on time and money) and *Happy Money Happy Life* (a book on happiness and money). It completes a trilogy I had envisioned many years ago.

The book in your hands is about *all things* money. It's a how-to guide sharing my step-by-step approach to achieving financial well-being. This book can stand on its own while incorporating the principles from my prior works. In some ways, it's an extension of my previous books, but it doesn't require you to have read them prior.

I could have written this book first, as it delves into the fundamental concepts of money. However, I firmly believe what stops our progress towards achieving goals is not the absence of steps but our mindset and habits. So, if you haven't read my previous books, I recommend adding them to your reading list.

Now, for those who've wanted step-by-step financial guidance from me, this book is for you. I have written all the necessary information you need to reach your financial goals and make your money smile.

With you on the journey,
Jason

Introduction

Make Your Money Smile is a how-to guide on personal finance. It's tactical and practical. The focus is to give you foundational financial knowledge and the steps to help you master money. Although this book will walk you step-by-step, you will see my philosophy on living a fulfilling life intertwined with the lessons. Because *money isn't the end goal; money is the tool to achieve the goals.*

I've written this book with an intention: to be your compassionate and empathetic guide. As someone who didn't start with a solid financial foundation, I made every money mistake you can think of. I had my share of ups and downs, twists and turns, and experienced the stress of being a high-achieving financial mess. I've also been judged. I've been ridiculed. But I persevered and triumphed. And I still managed a smile on my face.

I learned my way through the financial mess into personal success. I want to help you do the same. I will be your guide through it all. You'll learn the exact steps I took. You're also getting the knowledge of experts that I interviewed to help write this book, from money-savvy friends to sought-after financial experts.

Now, personal finance can be stressful when you don't know where to start. And a challenge to achieving financial well-being is figuring out what to do next. You see, our financial needs continue to evolve as we adapt to different life situations and world events. So the answer that helped you yesterday might not apply to your situation today. For instance, budgeting might have been the most challenging financial issue you faced in your 20s, but now you're stressing about investing in your 30s or about funding retirement in your 50s.

I've experienced that stress of trying to figure out what to do next. That's why I developed the Smile Money Pillars—a simple approach that places every aspect of personal finance into five pillars. Each pillar has three parts, broken into chapters, focusing on one aspect of money in actionable detail. You'll come away from each lesson with greater insight and takeaways to help you reach your goals. In this book, you'll learn the following.

Smile Money Pillars	Summary
Manage	Your **cash flow strategy** directs your money to what's most important.
Earn	Your **income strategy** optimizes your earnings and diversifies your income.
Grow	Your **investing strategy** prioritizes your savings for retirement and independence.
Borrow	Your **credit strategy** shifts your mindset to build wealth using leverage.
Protect	Your **legacy strategy** secures your most valuable assets.

I've been where you are, lost and confused, and unsure of where to start: it can be overwhelming. Or perhaps you're more money savvy and simply want to know if you've got all your bases covered. Whether you are the former or the latter, this book has something for everyone. It has something for you.

AN IMPORTANT MESSAGE

Before we get started, I want to acknowledge that your situation is unique. Certain variables affect your life that don't apply to other people. So when it comes to finding solutions to your financial situation, the answer will always start with "It depends." Because it does depend on a variety of factors that affect you specifically.

I'll be honest with you: I was never big on prescriptive financial advice. I don't believe in yelling at you to stop spending or shaming you about your debt. Doing so reduces us into mere caricatures devoid of the socioeconomic realities, systemic issues, and family structure and medical conditions that affect our financial decision-making. Personal finance is personal. And financial decisions aren't simply made with numbers. That said, this book will give you the financial framework that will revolutionize how you think, relate, and use money.

HOW TO USE THIS BOOK

I wrote this book with a purposeful flow.

I recommend reading the entire book to see what it offers. As you do, dog-ear page corners, add Post-it Notes, highlight sentences, mark up areas, and fill in the book in places I've asked questions. You can also use a journal or notepad on your smartphone to take notes. I encourage you to revisit the pillar(s) you want to work on more. This is your book. Make it yours and interact with it.

But feel free to skip around.

Do you need help with budgeting? Go to Chapter 2. Do you want to invest for financial independence? Skip to Chapter 9. Do you want to improve your credit score? Go to Chapter 11. Do you want to create your estate plan? Head on over to Chapter 15. You get the idea. Each chapter can stand independently. So go to where you need the most guidance.

Also, the book has an appendix that includes all the tables and exercises you'll see in the chapters. You can also download them and find all other resources shared on these pages by visiting thesmilemoney.com/book.

Are you ready to make your money smile? Let's go.

YOUR FINANCIAL WELL-BEING

We're about to explore a range of personal finance topics to enhance your financial know-how and steps to improve your financial well-being. But before we get into the pillars, let's begin with a financial checkup.

Financial Wellness Checkup

What areas need more of your attention? Circle your choice (Yes or No) and write down any thoughts that come to mind.

Do you feel generally optimistic about your finances? How you're feeling about your situation matters as it affects your health.	Yes / No
Do you know where your money is going? Using a budget or detailed knowledge of how you spend your money is essential.	Yes / No
Do you have an emergency fund? Having money to cover emergencies and unexpected expenses helps with peace of mind.	Yes / No
Do you have enough for monthly expenses? Your income should cover your needs, wants, and savings goals.	Yes / No
Have you recently paid any service fees? Paying bank fees, late fees, and nonsufficient funds (NSF) fees impacts your money.	Yes / No
Are you affording monthly debt payments? Debt should be minimized to reduce interest payments and improve cash flow.	Yes / No
Are you contributing to retirement? Take advantage of employer-sponsored plans and IRAs to fund your lifestyle in retirement.	Yes / No
Are you investing for independence? Invest money into a general investing account to regain your time freedom.	Yes / No
Do you have other forms of income? Don't rely solely on a paycheck. Income diversification is essential.	Yes / No
Do you have a healthcare plan? Health issues are the leading cause of financial stress.	Yes / No
Do you have a tax-saving strategy? Optimize your income withholding and reduce your future tax obligations.	Yes / No
Do you have life insurance? Protect your loved ones by giving them a safety net.	Yes / No
Do you have an estate plan? Indicate how you want your assets distributed.	Yes / No

(Continued)

Do you use all or most of your employee benefits? Use your salary and benefits to achieve goals.	Yes / No
Do you work with a money expert or a financial advisor? Get help and find answers to your specific financial situation and challenges.	Yes / No

How are you feeling? What are you thinking? This simple checkup increases your financial awareness. You'll notice areas of strengths and weaknesses. Note these areas, because they will be addressed in more detail in the following chapters.

Introducing the Smile Money Pillars

There are many parts to personal finance. It can feel overwhelming. At one point, I certainly was overwhelmed. So I started using a system that categorizes personal finance elements into five pillars, which I call the Smile Money Pillars. Each pillar focuses on a simple strategy:

1. **Manage Money.** The first pillar is your cash flow strategy, to direct your money to what's most important.

2. **Earn Money.** The second pillar is your income strategy, to optimize your earnings and diversify your income.

3. **Grow Money.** The third pillar is your investing strategy, to prioritize your savings for retirement and independence.

4. **Borrow Money.** The fourth pillar is your credit strategy, to shift your mindset to build wealth using leverage.

5. **Protect Money.** The fifth pillar is your legacy strategy, to secure your most valuable assets.

You don't have to master the pillars in order. The system is meant to help you organize your thoughts about money, making it simpler to reference an area of highest concern.

In the upcoming chapters, you'll discover straightforward steps to improve your finances. The best part? You can jump around or revisit specific pillars needing more of your attention. If you're keen on investing, go to the "Grow Money" section. To boost your earnings, skip to "Earn Money." Need to eliminate debt? Check out "Borrow Money." You get the point: you have the flexibility.

Okay, let's get started.

PILLAR I

Manage Money

*C*ash Flow Strategy

Tell your money where to go so it's spent on things that matter.

Managing money is more than just tracking numbers; it's about finding harmony between spending in the present and saving for the future. It's about enjoying today while securing a better financial tomorrow.

Let me start with a question: what came to mind when you read the words "manage money"?

Was it the "b" word? Did an image of a daunting task involving spreadsheets pop into your mind? Was it followed by a sigh of reluctance? Or were you happy because crunching numbers is your thing? While budgets are crucial for everyone whether you like or dislike them, I'm here to give you a different perspective. You need a budget, but it's not the rigid, restrictive concept you might think it is.

So if budgets actually work, why do people struggle with them? Well, there's a misconception that budgeting is about deprivation and it's thought of as a restrictive one-time task. Well, it isn't. In these chapters, you'll learn a better approach that changed my financial life and can change yours.

The first Smile Money pillar is Manage Money, the cash flow strategy.

Cash flow is about how your money moves in and out of your life. It's a critical aspect of personal finance because this is how you manage money. Here's a truth: the money you earn won't ever be enough if you don't know where your money goes and how to make it flow to where you want.

Mastering cash flow is the key to achieving financial goals. It determines success or failure in your financial wellness journey.

Manage Money	Direct where your money flows.

You make your money smile through cash flow management—how money enters and exits your life. It requires developing a budget that accounts for income, expenses, and savings goals. By embracing better spending habits and differentiating between needs and wants, you'll reach your life milestones.

In this pillar, you'll better understand banking concepts, how money works, the products and services to manage money well, and steps to cash flow your money. It features three lessons:

- **Lesson 1:** Elevate Your Banking Relationships
- **Lesson 2:** Create Your Budget
- **Lesson 3:** Cash Flow Your Money

Let's get managing!

CHAPTER 1

Elevate Your Banking Relationships

Contrary to popular belief, most people don't completely grasp banking. Sure, they know what it's for but don't truly understand how it works for them. And guess who benefits from this lack of knowledge? Certainly not you! The less you know, the more you pay in banking charges and fees.

The first lesson of the Manage Money pillar is understanding banking fundamentals, including financial institutions and their products and services. This might seem basic, but you must know them to manage your money better.

At its core, banking is both a financial service and a form of money management. Your banking accounts are the conduits through which your money flows, allowing you to perform financial transactions easily and conveniently. It's kind of like a car for your money. Just like a car takes you from place to place, bank accounts move your money from place to place too.

How does it all work? You can also think of banking as a game. Imagine yourself as a player in the banking game where there are two roles you can play: the saver and the borrower. Often, you find yourself in both positions simultaneously. As a saver, you might earn interest on your deposits, while as a borrower, you'll be required to pay interest on loans you take.

Now, banks, credit unions, and other financial institutions are masters at playing this game. They collect your deposits and then cleverly invest them, often through loans to other customers. It's a well-oiled machine that repeats over and over, allowing these institutions to make a profit and thrive.

To illustrate, say a bank offers a 1% interest on savings and offers a personal loan at an 8% interest rate. The difference between the 1% and 8% is the "spread" in which the financial institution makes its revenue for operational costs and profit.

In this chapter, you'll learn the following steps to elevate your banking relationships:

- **Step 1:** Using your banking accounts effectively
- **Step 2:** Identifying your ideal financial institution
- **Step 3:** Choosing your banking partner

STEP 1: USING YOUR BANKING ACCOUNTS EFFECTIVELY

The first step is understanding the common types of banking accounts available. Financial institutions offer different accounts for various purposes. And it's more than likely you'll need a few of these accounts to manage your money. So what kind of accounts do you have? Using the right banking accounts is vital because each one serves a purpose. Let's dive into the different banking accounts one by one.

Savings Accounts

A savings account is designed to help you save money for the future while earning some interest. It's a place to store your money, and the bank will pay you a small amount for keeping it with them.

Some banks may require a minimum deposit and may limit how often you can withdraw money or may charge fees for excessive withdrawals.

Checking Accounts

A checking account is a flexible transactional account that allows you to make deposits and withdrawals whenever you need to. It's handy for everyday spending and paying bills. While most checking accounts don't earn interest, some may offer a minimal interest rate. Be aware of transaction limits, minimum balance requirements, and fees associated with these accounts.

Debit Cards

A debit card is linked to your checking account and allows you to purchase conveniently at stores and online. You can spend only the amount of money in your account, which helps you manage your spending. Additionally, you can use your debit card at ATMs for deposits, withdrawals, balance reviews, and transfers between accounts.

Money Market Accounts (MMAs)

A money market account is a hybrid between savings and checking accounts. It typically requires a higher minimum balance and offers better interest rates than regular savings accounts. The interest rate may be fixed like a savings account or tied to financial market conditions.

Certificates of Deposit (CD)

A CD is a savings option with a fixed interest rate for a specific term, ranging from 30 days to several years. Your money is locked in for the agreed-upon period, and in return you earn a higher interest rate compared with a regular savings account.

Individual Retirement Accounts (IRA)

An IRA is a specialized savings account for retirement. There are two main types: traditional IRA and Roth IRA. Both offer tax advantages to help you grow your retirement savings. You can learn more about IRAs in the Grow Money pillar.

Remember, each account serves a different purpose, so use the ones that align with your needs and financial goals.

Now, let's talk strategy: choosing the right banking partner. Selecting the financial institution that best aligns with your needs and desires is fundamental. Be mindful because they are not created equal.

STEP 2: IDENTIFYING YOUR IDEAL FINANCIAL INSTITUTION

There are many types of financial institutions out there, each with its unique brand and offerings, giving you many options to choose from. First, there are the traditional banks that we all know, available in various sizes, from national giants to local community banks. Then there are credit unions, the not-for-profit champions, offering products and services like banks. And finally, there are alternative financial services available.

What kind of financial institution resonates with you? Let's go over the different types in more detail.

Banks

When we think of banking, we usually picture traditional banks. They come in different sizes, such as local, online, and national banks, and are regulated by state or federal agencies. The FDIC (Federal Deposit Insurance Corporation) protects the money you deposit in these banks, giving you peace of mind.

Credit Unions

Credit unions are another type of financial institution. They are not-for-profit organizations regulated by state or federal agencies. Like banks, they offer similar products and services, but due to their not-for-profit structure, they often provide better savings rates and lower loan interest. The NCUSIF (National Credit Union Share Insurance Fund) safeguards deposits of participating credit unions.

Online Banks

Online-only banks do everything through the internet, from account opening and management to transactions and customer support. Since they don't have physical branches, they can offer higher interest rates on savings accounts and lower fees for services, passing on the cost savings to their customers.

Alternative Financial Services

There are also financial companies known as neo-banks, mobile apps, and financial apps that provide banking services. Examples include prepaid debit cards and mobile payment apps. These alternative services may or may not have a banking charter but often work with traditional banks and credit unions to hold your deposits securely.

As you've read, there are many different types of financial institutions. And there are even more potential banking partners in each of those types. For instance, there are over 4,000 credit unions in the United States to choose from.

STEP 3: CHOOSING YOUR BANKING PARTNER

If you didn't know better, you might still be paying more for subpar banking services, paying unnecessary monthly fees, or using check-cashing services. Now that you know better, you can use a better banking partner. I want you to make a conscious effort and shop around.

- Consider banking locally with community banks and credit unions.
- Ask your family and friends what banking services they use.

Use the following questions to help narrow your banking choices:

- What's the company culture? Its mission?
- Where are they located?
- What products and services are available?
- Are there monthly or transactional fees?

- Are there minimum balance requirements?

- How can you access your money? What are the ATM network and fees?

- Can you set auto-transfers, auto-payments, and transaction alerts?

- Do you require a physical location (like a branch) or prefer a robust mobile app?

- Does community banking matter to you, or do you want the nationwide presence of a big bank?

- Are deposits FDIC or NCUSIF insured?

Take your time and explore your options to find the perfect match. And if you happen to choose a financial institution and learn it's not the right fit, find another. Again, you have options.

WHAT HAPPENS IF YOU GET DENIED A NEW BANKING ACCOUNT?

In some cases, a negative banking history can affect your ability to open new accounts. If, in the past, you've had multiple insufficient funds (NSFs), overdrawn accounts, or closed checking accounts because of abuse, these activities may be reported.

There are a few little-known consumer reporting agencies that many financial institutions use to determine if a new account should be opened. One such agency is ChexSystems, which collects and aggregates your banking history reported to them by participating financial institutions. It's similar to what credit bureaus do with your credit history.

There is good news: you can request a copy of your report, resolve outstanding issues, and dispute inaccuracies.

Under the Fair Credit Reporting Act (FCRA), you are entitled to a free copy of your ChexSystems consumer report, at your request, once every 12 months. And if you've been denied a new banking account and ChexSytems was used in the decision, you can also get a free consumer report.

If there's no information available in your report, it means you never had an adverse action reported by a financial institution. Additionally, you can dispute the inaccuracies if you find negative information in your report.

To request your consumer report, visit chexsystems.com.

TAKE ACTION

1. Review your existing banking relationships using the checklist in the Appendix.
2. Request a free copy of your ChexSystems consumer report.

 Elevate Your Banking Recap

In this chapter, you learned about banking fundamentals, the types of financial institutions available, and the products and services offered by them. The lessons presented the following steps:

- **Step 1:** Using your banking accounts effectively
- **Step 2:** Identifying your ideal financial institution
- **Step 3:** Choosing your banking partner

Remember, you have options when it comes to banking.

Congratulations! You've just finished your first lesson and elevated your banking knowledge. In the next chapter, you'll learn about budgets and the budgeting process that's best suited for you.

CHAPTER 2

Create Your Budget

Many people think of budgets as limiting themselves or as an act of deprivation. It's neither of those things. A budget is a framework to allocate your money into areas of your life, including expenses, debt, savings, and retirement goals. It's really that simple. A budget tells your money where to go, so you don't wonder where it went.

Let's get through some basics: a **budget** is a financial plan for a given period, like a monthly budget. It's a detailed outline of how you intend to allocate your income across various categories, such as housing, transportation, food, entertainment, savings, and more. The purpose of a budget is to set spending limits and financial goals, helping you to manage your money better.

For example, if you create a monthly budget that allocates $1000 for rent, $200 for groceries, $200 for transportation, $50 for entertainment, and $100 for savings, it becomes your budget for that specific month.

So what's in a budget? It includes the following:

- **Monthly income:** The total amount of money coming in from all sources
- **Monthly expenses:** Your monthly obligations like mortgage/rent, utilities, loan payments, and discretionary spending
- **Financial goals:** The monetarily quantifiable objectives like saving for an emergency, downpayment on a house, or vacation

Now, having a budget is not the same as budgeting. You see, **budgeting** is the process of creating and maintaining a budget. It involves planning, tracking, and managing your income and expenses based on your budget. For instance, if you spend time each month updating your budget, recording your income, and categorizing your expenses, you are budgeting.

In this chapter, you'll learn all about creating a budget in four steps:

- **Step 1:** Listing your income and expenses
- **Step 2:** Understanding your needs and wants
- **Step 3:** Choosing your budgeting method
- **Step 4:** Setting your financial goals

Let's get budgeting.

STEP 1: LISTING YOUR INCOME AND EXPENSES

You need to know what is coming in and what is going out. Assessing your monthly income and expenses is an important first step in creating a budget. You'll need to list the following:

- **Income** from salary, bonuses, tips, hourly wages, side hustles, self-employment, and investment sources.
- **Expenses** are necessary or optional spending that are paid monthly, including rent, mortgage, debt payments, utilities, groceries, streaming services, designer clothing, entertainment, and dining out.

Keep this in mind: the more detailed your expense list, the more you'll become aware of how your money is being used. It'll empower you to make crucial adjustments.

The following is an example of an income and expenses list. The worksheet is also available in the Appendix. Keep it handy because your income and expenses list will be used throughout the Smile Money Pillars.

Monthly Income and Expenses List*			
Income	**Amount**	**Expenses**	**Amount**
Salary	$3,500	Rent	$1500
Freelance work	$1,000	Utilities	$200
		Cell service	$95
		Student debt	$105
		Car loan	$350
Income Total	**$4,500**	**Expenses Total**	$2,250

See Appendix for the Monthly and Expenses List Worksheet.

STEP 2: UNDERSTANDING YOUR NEEDS AND WANTS

You might have noticed something after listing your income and expenses: perhaps you aren't making nearly enough to cover your lifestyle. Whether or not that is the case, it's vital to understand how you're spending money and if it's being used for things that make you smile.

Your spending will be used to meet either a need or a want. And there is a big difference between your needs and wants.

- **Needs are the essentials:** things you have to have to live life.
- **Wants are optional:** things you would like to have to enjoy life a *bit* more.

For example, you *need* a car to get to work, but you *want* a luxury vehicle. It's okay to want nice things. And I for one believe there is absolutely nothing wrong with wanting nicer things. The question you'll have to ask yourself is whether you can afford it without sacrificing other goals.

Look at your income and expenses list. Identify what expenses can be categorized as a need and what is a want. Use the Needs and Wants checklist to determine what's necessary and what's optional.

What Are Your Financial Needs?

Your needs are things that are essential, like shelter. It can also include obligations, like debt, which requires repayment.

✓	Needs Checklist
	Housing: Mortgage or rent
	Homeowner's or renter's insurance
	Property tax (if not already included in the mortgage payment)
	Auto insurance
	Health insurance
	Out-of-pocket healthcare costs, copayments, prescriptions
	Utilities: electrical, gas, water
	Internet
	Cell phone
	Life insurance
	Groceries and household goods
	Transportation: car, gas, tolls, public, rideshare
	Debt payments: student loans, installment loans
	Credit card balances: minimum payments
	Other loans: monthly payments
	Child support or alimony payments
	Wellness programs: gym membership
	Care: childcare, adult care, daycare

What Are Your Financial Wants?

Your wants are things that are nice to have but aren't necessary. However, they might be essential to improving your quality of life. For instance, it's not necessary to dine at restaurants, but you may want to.

✓	Wants checklist
	Entertainment: movies, events, concerts
	Clothing
	Dining out

✓	Wants checklist
	Prepaid meals and food delivery
	Conventions and conferences
	Subscriptions: news, streaming shows, music
	Travel: airline tickets, hotels, rental cars, etc.
	Cable and home phone
	Additional perks: cell phone insurance

STEP 3: CHOOSING YOUR BUDGETING METHOD

After listing your income and expenses and understanding your needs and wants, it's time to reallocate your money to what's important. It's time to choose your budget.

There are many different ways to budget your money, from buckets to envelope systems to software programs. You have options. My personal choice is a method I shared in my book *You Only Live Once*, which is closely related to zero-based budgeting. You'll learn how to do this in the next chapter, "Cash Flow Your Money."

With zero-based budgeting, you must identify and track each expense. The goal is to have your income minus your expenditures equal to zero by the end of the month. It allocates all of your money to expenses, savings, and debt payments.

DIFFERENT BUDGET METHODS

The best budget is the one you use. And you're in luck. There are many types of budgets you can use. Some of the popular ones include the following:

50-30-20 Rule

The rule allocates your paycheck into three areas:

- 50% for essentials like mortgage or rent, utilities, groceries, etc.
- 30% for nonessentials like dining out, clothing, streaming services, other subscriptions, etc.

(Continued)

(Continued)

■ 20% for savings goals like an emergency fund, retirement contributions, credit card and loan payments, etc.

80-20 Rule

This simpler plan directs 20% of your paycheck towards savings goals. It leaves 80% for everything else, from the necessary to discretionary. For instance, as your income grows, so does the amount of money saved because you're always saving 20%.

Cash-Only Plan

With a cash-only budget, you're only using cash, which means no credit or debit cards or even checks. Basically, you're choosing to opt out of technology. This is often used with the envelope budget system, where you place cash for expenses in separate envelopes. Once you run out of cash, you stop spending. This is for the very tactile person who needs to feel the cash leave their hands.

What Method Is Right for You?

It really depends on your preferences. Any of these budgets can help you achieve your goals. Again, a budget is only useful if you adhere to it.

STEP 4: SETTING YOUR FINANCIAL GOALS

Setting your financial goals is necessary so you can begin to direct money towards them. What financial goals do you currently have? What goals came up as you listed your income and expenses? It's possible you identified goals like paying off debt, saving for an emergency, owning a home, and going on a dream vacation. Remember, your goals are going to be specific to your own personal situation and desires.

Make Your Financial Goals SMART

Having goals is necessary, and making them SMART is vital in achieving them. I want you to use the SMART method to guide you. (SMART stands for specific, measurable, attainable, relevant, time-bound.)

A SMART goal is saying, "I will save $2,500 over the next 10 months by setting aside $250 each month from my paycheck. This allows me to enjoy my vacation in Mexico during the holidays and cover my flight, food, hotel, and activities." In contrast, a non-SMART goal is "I want to save money for a trip to Mexico." Use SMART goals.

SMART Goals*	
Specific goals have a much greater chance of being reached.	What do you want to accomplish? Is the goal clearly defined and specific?
Measurable goals track your progress and help you stay motivated.	How much do you need? Can progress towards the goal be quantified or measured?
Attainable goals show what you can control based on your resources and skills.	How can you accomplish this goal? Is the goal realistic and attainable within the given limits?
Relevant goals ensure they align with your values.	What can and will you do? Does the goal align with broader objectives and priorities?
Timely goals have a deadline or target date.	When do you want it? What is the deadline or time frame for achieving the goal?

Let's say a financial goal is going on vacation. Use SMART for clarity.

Specific	I am saving money for a vacation.
Measurable	$2500
Attainable	I can transfer $100.00 per paycheck.
Relevant	It supports my mental health by taking time off.
Time-bound	I'll reach the savings goal in 12 months.

*See Appendix for the SMART Goals Worksheet.

You can also use SMART goals for debt payoff.

Specific	I will pay off my credit card debt.
Measurable	$5,000
Attainable	I will pay $450.00 monthly towards the debt.
Relevant	This relieves the stress I feel and will help me start contributing more for retirement.
Time-bound	I will pay it off in 12 months.

What are your goals? Write them down. You'll need these goals so you can direct the flow of money to them. Let's do an exercise. Identify one goal and write it down in this table.

Specific	
Measurable	
Attainable	
Relevant	
Time-bound	

TAKE ACTION

Use the worksheets in the Appendix to help you complete the exercises from this lesson.

1. List your income and expenses using the worksheet.
2. Complete the Needs and Wants checklist.
3. Identify three financial goals using the SMART method.

 Create Your Budget Recap

In the chapter, you learned that a budget is vital to financial well-being. If you don't know how much you're truly making and how you're spending it, you'll experience a greater amount of financial stress. The lessons presented the following steps:

- **Step 1:** Listing your income and expenses
- **Step 2:** Understanding your needs and wants
- **Step 3:** Choosing your budgeting method
- **Step 4:** Setting your financial goals

Remember, budgeting is a process helping you get from where you are to where you want to be.

You did it! Congrats on completing the lesson in budgeting better. In the next chapter, you'll learn how to successfully use the cash flow method.

CHAPTER **3**

Cash Flow
Your Money

I want you to think about cash flow because it helps you make informed decisions and ensure you have the necessary funds to cover your expenses and meet your financial goals. It goes beyond budgeting. And whether or not you've used a budget before, it truly is just the beginning, not the whole system. It might be helpful to think of managing money in this way:

1. A financial plan is a roadmap to your goals.
2. A budget allocates your income to expenses and goals.
3. Cash flow is how you move money into and out of your life.

With the cash flow strategy, you intentionally direct money to flow into the areas that are most important to you. There are six steps:

- **Step 1:** Calculating your cash flow number
- **Step 2:** Analyzing your flow
- **Step 3:** Spending less of your money

- **Step 4:** Saving more of your income
- **Step 5:** Automating your finances
- **Step 6:** Choosing your expense-tracking app

You will learn to say "yes" to the things that matter.

Unfortunately, most financial advice is about saying "no." No to dinners. No to friends. No to this or that. No to everything you enjoy. It's demotivating and unrealistic. Basically, mainstream advice amounts to experts yelling at you for not spending money like them.

I'm here to show you how to say "yes" to what truly matters. The cash flow method will help you do just that.

Let's start flowing.

STEP 1: CALCULATING YOUR CASH FLOW NUMBER

Why is it important to calculate monthly cash flow? It's a strong indicator of financial health. Calculating your cash flow number involves understanding where your money comes from and where it goes. It determines if you're living at, below, or above your means. Basically, you're subtracting your expenses from your income. I'm sure you're recognizing the similarity of listing income and expenses when creating a budget.

I want you to refer to your income and expenses list to calculate your cash flow. Use the following equation:

Cash Flow = Net Monthly Income (Money In) – Monthly Expenses

What's Your Net Monthly Income?

Your primary source of income might be the salary and wages from an employer. But your income includes bonuses, side hustles, rental property, interest or investment income, government checks, or any other source. Gross monthly income (pre-tax) is how much you earn. Your net monthly income is your take-home pay (after taxes).

Income List*	Net Monthly Income Example	Your Net Monthly Income
Salary	$4,300	$
Other Income:_____	$1,000	$
Total Income	**$5,300**	**$**

*See Appendix for the Income List Worksheet.

You'll need your monthly net income from all sources to calculate cash flow. You'll learn more about increasing, multiplying, and diversifying your income sources in the Earn Money pillar.

What Are Your Expenses?

Listing your personal and household expenses is an integral step in managing your money. Here is a sample list of expenses:

- Cost of housing (mortgage/rent)
- Utilities (water, electric, gas)
- Subscriptions (cell service, streaming services)
- Insurance (auto, home, life, renters, pet)
- Dining and entertainment
- Groceries and household supplies
- Home and car maintenance
- Transportation (car payments, fuel cost, tolls, tickets, public transport)
- Healthcare (copays, over-the-counter medicine, prescriptions)
- Debt such as a credit card or personal loans
- Expense of paying yourself first

Typically, most financial experts will talk about fixed and variable expenses. Fixed expenses are the same monthly payments like rent, mortgage, car payments, subscriptions, and installment loans. Variable expenses change monthly. The amount billed fluctuates based on usage. It includes utilities, car and home maintenance, gas, food, and entertainment.

However, I've learned that people don't think in fixed or variable categories. Instead, using bills, debts, and optional categories might be easier. It's what I refer to as your BDO expenses.

Bills	are necessary expenses, needed, or essential to living. This includes your monthly mortgage or rent, insurance premiums, utilities, transportation, food, subscriptions, and credit card payments.
Debts	are fixed financial obligations such as student loans, car loans, and unsecured loans. They include optional expenses you financed with required monthly payments.
Optional	expenses aren't necessary or an obligation. They are entirely discretionary and include clothing, dining, entertainment, trips, and subscriptions.

As part of the cash flow strategy, you'll list all BDO expenses to understand how you spend your paycheck. I've also included savings goals as an expense (e.g., paying yourself first). Here is an expense worksheet.

Expense List*	Monthly Expense Example	Your Monthly Expense
Bills		
Rent	$1,500	$
Electricity	$200	$
Transportation	$200	$
Groceries	$300	$
Cell service	$75	$
Debt		
Mortgage	$0	$
Car loan	$350	$
Credit card	$100	$
Student loan	$150	$
Optional		
Clothing	$50	$
Entertainment	$50	$
Subscriptions	$50	$
Dining	$100	$
Savings Goals		
Rainy Day	$25	$

Expense List*	Monthly Expense Example	Your Monthly Expense
Opportunity Fund	$25	$
Car downpayment	$0	$
Total	**$3,175**	$

See Appendix for the Expense List Worksheet.

What's Your Cash Flow?

It's now time to put the numbers together. Do the math: subtract your expenses from your income.

Net Monthly Income (Money In) – Monthly Expenses (Money Out) = Cash Flow

	Income (Money In)	Minus	Expenses (Money Out)	Equals	Cash Flow
Cash Flow Example	$5,300	–	$3,175	=	$2,125
Your Cash Flow	$	–	$	=	$

And that's how you get your cash flow number. The example shows a positive cash flow number, signifying financial health. The next step is analyzing your number.

STEP 2: ANALYZING YOUR FLOW

You've probably heard the personal finance advice to "live within your means." It means to live without overspending. However, many people don't know what their "means" are because they haven't done the work to calculate their cash flow.

Well, you've just done the work. Now, determine whether you live within, above, or below your means.

- Living **within** your means is spending your income with nothing left over.
- Living **above** your means is spending more than your income.
- Living **below** your means is spending less than your income.

How are you living?

Cash Flow Analysis: How are you living? (circle one)	
Within	You're doing well, but it might lead to future financial trouble if unexpected expenses arise or income is disrupted.
Above	You're living on borrowed money, which means you're experiencing a great deal of financial stress.
Below	You're financially healthy and can treat yourself a bit while contributing more towards your goals.

Why Is It Important to Analyze Your Cash Flow Monthly?

Let's say your income includes full-time and freelance work. Here's how it can play out.

In a month of positive cash flow, you have $2,125 left after subtracting expenses from your take-home pay of $5,300. The "leftover" money can be used to accelerate funding your savings goals, pay off debt, or invest in your future.

However, not all months are the same. For instance, your freelance gig ended and reduced your take-home income to $4,300. You also had an unexpected expense of $3,000 when your furnace needed to be replaced. Your expense for that month is $6,175, leaving you with a negative cash flow of $1,875. Not having enough income to cover the expenses or savings to dip into can lead to using credit to cover the shortfall.

Calculating your cash flow monthly can help accelerate savings goals in positive net worth months. And by doing so, it can help cover a shortfall during negative cash flow months.

STEP 3: SPENDING LESS OF YOUR MONEY

After analyzing your cash flow, determine the non-value-added expenses. This will help you determine what can be eliminated or reduced. In this step, you'll need to review your BDO expense list.

Remember, your essential expenses relate to housing, food, and healthcare. In some cases, optional purchases can be essential in your life because they give you joy. For instance, I like my Starbucks

Frappuccinos and coffeehouse brews. I am okay with spending on coffee because I enjoy it. What I do differently than others is how I intentionally spend less in one area to enjoy my small cups of joy. I have in the past cut out coffee purchases for an entire year to save more money to reach a travel goal faster.

Here's the thing: small purchases can add up, making larger goals all the more challenging to achieve. Also, small purchases often creep up without you even realizing it. So a cup of coffee a day can lead to two or more. That's when cash flowing your money is vital to success. You'll recognize how your spending is aligned with your goals. You'll see how it's changing monthly. And it'll help you adjust accordingly.

Using my coffee example, if you buy coffee every day and aren't someone who finds joy in it, then choose to make coffee at home. And, of course, you can take a trip to the coffeehouse occasionally as a treat.

You see, when you spend on too many things with no true value, you inevitably create a future when you cannot afford what's truly valuable.

I want you to cut out the things that don't add value. And you're in luck, because it's up to you to determine what purchases aren't adding value. So instead of eliminating $5 coffees, you could consider reducing housing expenses, eliminating cable, consolidating debt, and so on. These expenses could lead to hundreds of dollars in savings per month.

Now, look at your BDO list to identify the expenses to eliminate, negotiate, reduce, and consolidate.

Eliminate

Cut expenses and cancel unnecessary plans altogether. For example, if you have a gym membership you don't use, cancel it. Perhaps you're paying for multiple streaming services; choose one service and eliminate the rest. If you can't eliminate a plan, remove add-ons and extras to reduce the monthly cost.

Negotiate

Call your service providers and negotiate your service contracts. Ask about cheaper options for the service you already have with them.

Consider your utilities, home and auto insurance, smartphone data, and subscriptions. Ask about group or affiliate discounts, too.

When negotiating, it's best to know what other providers offer, so shop around. Use that knowledge tactfully when speaking with a customer service rep. Consider switching if you cannot get a matching price or a lower amount.

Reduce

Review your spending on groceries, dining, entertainment, clothing, and trips. You probably don't need to eliminate items that support a healthy lifestyle, but reduce the amount you spend. I like using online coupons and cashback websites. Some people think it takes too much effort, but these apps and websites make it easy to spend less. The small amounts can add up nicely, too.

Consolidate

What expenses can you consolidate? Can you join someone's cell phone plan? Could you share streaming service plans with a friend? Does an umbrella insurance policy reduce your premiums? Is it possible to consolidate your debt for lower monthly payments? Think outside the box and get really creative.

Now, I want you to think about your spending. Review the expense list and write down in this matrix the expenses you can eliminate, negotiate, reduce, and consolidate.

Spend Less Matrix*	
Eliminate	Negotiate
Reduce	Consolidate

*See Appendix for the Spend Less Matrix.

I want you to highlight this: there is only so much you can cut out before you start depriving yourself of the small joys. Be flexible and allow yourself room for little purchases.

And one more thing: while you're limited in how many expenses you can cut, your income-earning potential is unlimited. You'll learn different ways to increase your income in the Earn Money pillar.

6 TIPS TO LOWER YOUR EXPENSES

Tip 1. Lower grocery and household expenses

Don't spend more than you need on necessities such as food and cleaning supplies. Use coupons, discount codes, and cashback apps.

Tip 2. Lower your cell phone bill

Call your cellular provider and ask about new promotions and discounts. Can you switch to a different plan? Can you add an employer or association discount? If you're out of contract, consider switching carriers to lower your bill. You can do this every year or so.

Tip 3. Lower cable, internet, and home phone bills

Ask your existing provider about lowering the monthly bill. Negotiate with the representative and consider cutting the cord or removing the home phone line. If necessary, switch providers.

Tip 4. Lower electric and other utility bills

Many utility companies offer credits or payment options to lower your monthly bill. Request information on how to lower your monthly bills. Some ways include changing thermostat settings and fixing a dripping faucet, which can lower utility costs.

Tip 5. Lower subscription costs

Limit the number of subscriptions you have. Consider canceling streaming services, food delivery, a newspaper or newsletter, a money app, and a credit monitoring service. Or find a cheaper alternative or choose a lower subscription tier.

(Continued)

(Continued)

Tip 6: Lower insurance expense

Don't assume your loyalty guarantees the best auto insurance rate for your situation. Insurance carriers may consider you price-optimized and incrementally increase your rates. Shopping around lets them know you're ready to leave and makes them more agreeable to lowering premiums.

   To find apps and services to help you spend less, visit the resource page at thesmilemoney.com/book.

STEP 4: SAVING MORE OF YOUR INCOME

Make your money goals an expense and "pay yourself first."

Paying yourself first means saving money every time you get paid. Saving money can be considered "spending" because you put money aside for future expenses. Think of yourself as a bill and allocate money into a savings account each and every payday. Have your paycheck directly deposited into your checking account, and automatically transfer a portion of your income into a savings account.

Don't know what savings account to have? Start with the purposeful savings plan.

Purposeful Savings Plan

I first introduced the purposeful savings plan in *You Only Live Once*. Separating my savings into different accounts was a game-changer for my finances. It kept me from withdrawing money for purchases unrelated to my goals and made me more accountable to them.

With the purposeful savings plan, you save for emergencies and as well as for short-, mid-, and long-term goals. You'll want multiple savings accounts to help prioritize important goals and track progress. This savings plan is about being specific on how your money will be used. The plan has five specific savings goals:

- **Rainy Day Fund** helps you cover expenses related to unforeseen events. I suggest having the equivalent of your auto insurance deductible. For example, if your auto insurance deductible is $500, have $500 in your rainy day fund. After using the money to cover expenses, replenish the fund.

- **Happy Fund** is one month's salary for wellness activities. It can be used for vacations, a long weekend getaway, massages, or self-care.

- **Opportunity Fund** helps you cover basic living expenses if you lose your job, your hours are reduced, or you become sick, disabled, or hospitalized for a period of time. It's called an opportunity fund because you regain the time you once spent at work to rest and explore new opportunities. It's about six months of basic living expenses.

- **Freedom Fund** is savings to cover your living expenses for an entire year. Freedom is the opportunity to take a sabbatical to explore new interests or spend time with loved ones. I highly recommend a planned year off in the middle of your career.

- **Cash reserve** is savings for your financial security for periods of economic uncertainty and stock market volatility. Cash reserves are 24 months of basic living expenses.

A note about "basic living expenses." These are your needs: the essential and necessary expenses each month. Understand that the lower your expenses, the lower the amount needed in the funds. For example, if your living expenses are $4,000 each month, then you'll need $24,000 in your Opportunity Fund. If basic living expenses are only $2,000, your savings goal is reduced to $12,000 for that fund.

You might think these are too many funds to keep track of. I've learned that identifying the purpose of our savings is what often helps us achieve them.

What about Other Savings Goals?

Other savings-type goals include home downpayment, car purchase, travel, and holiday gift expenses. Review the financial goals you identified when creating your budget. Turn those goals into an expense so you can "pay" into them with each paycheck.

Having specific and separate savings accounts for each goal will help you save.

- **Prioritize the most important goals:** Having multiple savings accounts helps you visualize your important goals. Each time you log into your accounts, you can quickly see why you're saving. It will become harder to withdraw money from one account to spend on something else.

- **Track progress:** It's easier to track savings progress with separate accounts. The main reason is that you can visually see how you're progressing. The visual cues are a reminder to keep contributing.

- **Individual targeted goals:** For example, if your Rainy Day Fund goal is $500 and your car fund goal is $5,000, separating them into different accounts can make it easier to achieve your goals.

The great thing is that you can have a savings account for each of your goals. Title the accounts accordingly. Edit a generically named "savings account" into a purposeful savings account: "$1,000 for rainy days." Naming each account for its intended purpose reminds you of your why—the reason for saving. Doing so keeps you from dipping into them for unrelated expenses.

Complete this worksheet to start your purposeful savings plan.

Purposeful Savings Plan*	Goal	Amount Needed	Monthly Contribution
Rainy Day Fund	$1000	$	$
Happy Fund	1-month salary for wellness, vacation	$	$
Opportunity Fund	6 months of basic living expenses	$	$
Freedom Fund	12 months of living expenses	$	$
Cash Reserve	24 months of living expenses	$	$

*See Appendix for the Purposeful Savings Worksheet.

Many banks and credit unions offer multiple savings accounts. If your financial institution does not, find another banking partner that does.

I want you to know that successfully saving money for future spending is about motivation. Choose whether you want to save money in each fund, or focus on reaching one fund goal before moving on to the next.

My experience has taught me that focusing on one savings goal at a time helps me reach all my goals. You certainly can fund each savings account every payday. But if you're the type who wants to see progress, focus on funding one goal first, then move on to the next.

But what if you want simplicity?

Some people like having all their savings in one big savings account. I've done this before, and it didn't work well for me. You might be different and want the minimalism of fewer accounts. In that case, my only caution is to ensure you're a mindful saver and an intentional spender.

STEP 5: AUTOMATING YOUR FINANCES

Free yourself from the mundane and tedious parts of managing money. I'm a big advocate of automating your finances. This frees up your mental bandwidth and your time. It also helps you reach goals with less effort. So make it easier on yourself and automate as much of your finances as possible.

Contrary to popular belief, you don't have to do manual work to manage money. The truth is that automating finances supports good habits and helps you reach your financial goals.

Do the following for successful money management:

- **Start with the right checking account.** Use the best banking product with automation tools (auto-transfers, spending alerts, and so on).
- **Enroll in direct deposit.** Deposit your entire net pay into your checking account. You'll need to set this up with your employer. Also, don't forget to automate your retirement savings. Set your 401(k) retirement plan contributions. (You'll learn more about this in the Grow Money pillar.)
- **Create auto-transfer rules.** Automate savings with a set amount transferred each payday to your funds.

- **Set up auto-bill pay.** Don't forget another bill and opt-in for automatic minimum payments to avoid pesky late fees.
- **Enroll in e-statements.** Forget the paper and have your statements emailed to you each month.
- **Use an expense-tracking tool.** You don't need a spreadsheet. Automate the categorization of your spending with expense-tracking software. I'll cover this in the next step.

Use this worksheet to help you automate your finances.

Automation Checklist*	Date Completed
Completed review of primary checking account	
Enrolled in direct deposit	
Enrolled in e-statements	
Contributions to employer-sponsored retirement plans set	
Purposeful savings funds: auto-savings transfers set	
Other savings accounts: auto-savings transfers set	
Mortgage or rent: auto-payment set	
Utilities: auto-payments set	
Utilities: auto-payments set	
Cell phone services: auto-payment set	
Credit cards: auto-payments set	
Student loans: auto-payments set	
Other debts: auto-payments set	

*See Appendix for the Automation Checklist.

STEP 6: CHOOSING YOUR EXPENSE-TRACKING APP

Expenses have a way of creeping into our lives and can derail us from achieving goals. It happened to me and there's a good chance it'll happen to you as well.

To reach your goals, you must track your spending.

You can track your expenses manually by downloading your monthly statements and inputting expenses into a spreadsheet. Or you can automate and use an expense-tracking app that does the work for you. Automating tracking helps you see spending categories more easily, spot potential issues earlier, and adjust spending sooner.

Expense-tracking software has come a long way. However, you'll need to do minor things, such as adjusting specific purchases to align with the right categories. Remember, expense-tracking apps only track purchases made to linked financial accounts such as checking accounts and credit or debit cards.

The good news is that you have options when it comes to expense-tracking apps. Your bank might even offer one already integrated with your accounts. Or you can download a free or paid app with more robust features. Find the most updated and best expense-tracking tools by visiting thesmilemoney.com/book.

TAKE ACTION

Use the worksheets in the Appendix to help you complete the exercises in this lesson.

1. Calculate your monthly cash flow using the Income and Expenses worksheet.
2. Analyze your cash flow number and determine how you're living.
3. Complete the Spend Less Matrix.
4. Start your Rainy Day Fund from the purposeful savings plan.
5. Complete the Automation Checklist.
6. Download an expense-tracking app.

 Cash Flow Your Money Recap

Analyzing your numbers can encourage you to find ways to diversify your income and make adjustments to expenses. The lessons learned featured six steps:

- **Step 1:** Calculating your cash flow number
- **Step 2:** Analyzing your flow

(*Continued*)

(Continued)

> ▪ **Step 3:** Spending less of your money
> ▪ **Step 4:** Saving more of your income
> ▪ **Step 5:** Automating your finances
> ▪ **Step 6:** Choosing your expense-tracking app
>
> Remember, the cash flow strategy is about intentionally directing money to flow into the areas most important to you. It's also about making your financial life easier.

MANAGE MONEY SUMMARY

You've just completed the Manage Money pillar. In these chapters, you strengthened your banking and budgeting knowledge, and mastered the cash flow strategy to direct where your money goes. The pillar comprised three lessons:

▪ **Lesson 1:** Elevate Your Banking Relationships

▪ **Lesson 2:** Create Your Budget

▪ **Lesson 3:** Cash Flow Your Money

Here's an important note: once you have the strategy in place and, perhaps, customized to your lifestyle, you'll come to grasp that you don't need to be on top of your finances every day. You now have systems in place to alert you of issues and prepare you for the unexpected. This is how you make your money smile: you're managing money; it's not managing you.

Congrats again on mastering the Manage Money pillar. It's now time to increase your earnings. In the next pillar, Earn Money, you'll learn how to optimize your paycheck, get a pay raise, and multiply and diversify your income.

PILLAR II

Earn Money

*I*ncome Strategy

You deserve more money.

The good news is that there are many ways to make money flow into your life. Better yet, there are different ways to earn more without exchanging more time for a paycheck. I want you to know that income can be earned by exchanging your time, skill, labor, capital, or service. It can also be earned through a business, rental properties, or stock investments. Your path to living well is by opening the income gates, allowing money to flow in more easily. This is how you make your money smile.

The second pillar is Earn Money—your income strategy. It's about increasing your wages from a job, multiplying your income, and creating passive income sources.

| Earn Money | Optimize your earnings, and diversify and multiply your income. |

Some people have wondered how I make a living. They know I'm an author and entrepreneur but don't exactly know how I can afford my lifestyle. The reality is that I don't depend on just one income. I have multiple income streams.

My income flows primarily from speaking and consulting gigs, and I earn royalties from my books, my writing on publishing platforms like medium.com, and videos posted on Facebook and YouTube. I also make money as the owner of multiple websites. And on rare occasions, I work as a spokesperson or brand ambassador with company brands. The active income earned is then invested into passive streams such as dividend-paying stocks, real estate investment trusts (REITs), and crowdfunded loans. I also earn money through interest on savings accounts and certificates of deposit (CDs).

I know from experience that there are still many more ways for income to flow into my life. And I know there are many ways income can flow into yours.

In the following chapters, you'll learn the 3-5-7 PRIME method:

- **Lesson 1:** Optimize Your Paycheck (3)
- **Lesson 2:** Multiply Your Income Streams (5)
- **Lesson 3:** Diversify Your Income Sources (7)

PRIME stands for Passive Recurring Income for More Earnings. It's a mouthful, and I don't expect you to remember it. The method emphasizes the importance of passive income to reach a work-optional lifestyle.

Let's get earning!

CHAPTER **4**

Optimize Your Paycheck

For many, the primary income source is from a job. And there's a good chance your money is primarily made by working for someone else too. Your first Earn Money lesson is to learn how to increase your pay at a job without working more hours. In fact, there are several things you can do, including negotiating a higher salary, seeking promotions, or, if that fails, finding a new job that pays more. Before you go seeking new employment, let's go over how to optimize your current earnings.

First, I want to go over paycheck fundamentals. A paycheck is how you get paid and is attached to a paystub that typically contains a number of elements:

- **Employee information:** This can include your name, address, Social Security number (often redacted), and employee ID number.
- **Gross pay:** This is the total amount of money you earn before any deductions.
- **Net pay:** This is the amount of money you take home after all deductions, such as taxes, retirement contributions, and insurance premiums, have been taken out.

- **Taxes:** This section shows the federal, state, and local taxes withheld from your paycheck.
- **Social Security and Medicare:** This section shows the amount of money withheld from your paycheck for Social Security and Medicare taxes, referred to as FICA.
- **Deductions:** This section shows any other pre-tax contributions and deductions taken from your paycheck, such as contributions to a retirement plan or health insurance premiums.
- **Hours worked:** This section shows the number of hours you worked during the pay period.
- **Pay period:** This is the period for which you are paid, such as weekly, biweekly, or monthly.
- **Pay date:** This is the date you will receive your paycheck.
- **Employer information:** This includes the name and address of your employer, as well as the employer identification number.

One of the most important things to understand is the difference between gross pay and net pay. The gap between the two is often a cause of stress for people. It's possible you've said, "They're taking *how much* from my check?!"

I want you to think of this gap differently. There are some things you can control to narrow the gap. And in this chapter, you'll learn to make different choices to optimize your earnings. The number three in the 3-5-7 PRIME method refers to the three specific ways to optimize your earnings:

- **Step 1:** Improving your net pay through deductions and contributions
- **Step 2:** Maximizing your earnings using employer benefits
- **Step 3:** Making more at your current job

STEP 1: IMPROVING YOUR NET PAY THROUGH DEDUCTIONS AND CONTRIBUTIONS

If you're like me, you might have been angry once or twice during payday because of the amount of money taken from your gross pay. Here's the thing: many people simply accept it rather than learn how to optimize their paycheck. There are things you can do such as adjusting your tax withholdings, using deductions, and increasing contributions. Doing so might actually have a positive impact on your earnings.

Adjusting Your Tax Withholding

I asked a friend, Yaroslav Tashak, CPA and founder of CPA-gurus.com, about ways to optimize our paychecks. His initial response was that most people don't know how to fill in their W-4s correctly. This could lead to a much bigger refund, or an income tax bill.

The W-4 form is the document you complete to tell your employer how much federal taxes to withhold from your paycheck. But it's also the form that's used to make adjustments at any time.

Adjusting the information on the W-4 changes the amount of tax withheld and impacts your take-home pay. Yaroslav shared the importance of adjusting the withholding after life events like marriage, having children, or getting a second job or side hustle. He added that most people forget to do this, which can lead to higher tax bills.

If you want to see how adjusting your W-4 can impact your take-home pay, check out the tax withholding calculator on the IRS website, irs.gov, or visit thesmilemoney.com/book.

Using Pre-Tax Contributions

Pre-tax contributions are taken from your income before taxes are calculated. It can lower your taxable income and potentially reduce the amount of taxes you owe.

"I recommend people take advantage of any pre-tax benefits employers offer," Yaroslav explained, adding, "These are expenses you will end up spending money on regardless, so you might as well get a tax benefit from them."

Some of the most common pre-tax contributions include retirement plans, health savings accounts, transportation, and childcare. Use the checklist to assess what pre-tax contributions you're using.

✓	Common Pre-Tax Contributions Checklist	
	401(k) Contributions	The money you contribute to a 401(k) retirement plan is deducted before taxes, helping you save for retirement while reducing your taxable income.
	Health Insurance Premiums	If your employer offers health insurance, your premiums are often deducted pre-tax, making it more affordable to maintain coverage.
	Flexible Spending Account (FSA)	Money contributed to an FSA for medical expenses, dependent care, or transportation costs is taken out of your paycheck before taxes.
	Health Savings Account (HSA)	Contributions to an employer's HSA plan are pre-tax. It's used for qualified medical expenses and can be used to cover eligible healthcare costs.
	Transportation Commuter Benefits	If your employer provides commuter benefits for public transportation or qualified parking expenses, the amount is deducted pre-tax.
	Dental and Vision Insurance Premiums	Like health insurance, premiums for dental and vision coverage can often be deducted before taxes.
	Group Life Insurance Premiums	If your employer offers group life insurance, the premiums may be deducted pre-tax.
	Qualified Tuition Assistance	Some employers offer tuition assistance or reimbursement programs, and the benefits are typically pre-tax.
	Qualified Adoption Assistance	If you're adopting a child, certain adoption-related expenses can be deducted pre-tax.
	Union Dues	If you're a union member, your dues may be taken from your paycheck before taxes.
	Legal Assistance Plans	Some employers offer pre-tax deductions for legal assistance plans.
	Retirement Savings for Self-Employed	If you're self-employed, contributions to individual retirement accounts (IRAs) can be deducted before taxes.

Remember that the answer to your tax situation starts with "it depends." The availability of these pre-tax contributions may vary depending on your personal situation, employer's benefits package, and federal and state tax laws. It's essential to consult with a tax professional to understand how these benefits apply to your situation.

How Pre-Tax Contributions and Deductions Impact Your Earnings

The difference between a pre-tax contribution and a deduction is when they affect your income and taxes. A **pre-tax contribution** is money taken from your salary before taxes are paid. It reduces your taxable income, so you end up paying fewer taxes overall. In contrast, a **deduction** is an eligible expense that's subtracted from your taxable income (after pre-tax contributions have been taken out).

Here's what you really need to know: Optimize your earnings by taking advantage of pre-tax contributions to reduce your taxable income. And use deductions to lower your tax bills when filing your income tax returns. You'll learn more about tax planning in the Protect Money pillar.

STEP 2: MAXIMIZING YOUR EARNINGS WITH EMPLOYER BENEFITS

I understand how common it is to think only about the money that is directly deposited into our checking accounts. But I want you to be uncommon. It's also about how much potential "earnings" you're missing out on by not using your benefits.

Don't leave money on the table.

If you're not using the perks and benefits offered by your employer, you're saying no to "free" money. Basically, you're saying "no thanks" to benefits that belong to you. Don't do that. There are financial benefits when using them.

In the last company I worked for, we had some really cool benefits and perks. I would get a $25 gift card for every health and wellness workshop I attended, up to $250 annually. I used the tuition reimbursement of up to $5,250 per calendar year to pay for my continuing education. I also took advantage of the gym membership discount, bicycle commuting credit, and cell phone discounts to lower my expenses, which amounted to $200 in monthly savings.

I want you to think about the benefits offered by your employer. Consider the associated financial gains you're missing out on.

Here's a prime example: people who don't contribute to 401(k) plans and miss out on employer-matching contributions. It saddens me because this is money that belongs to you. It's money you're opting not to receive. And it's money you'll come to need during your retirement years.

Other examples include underutilized benefits such as flexible spending accounts or health savings accounts (that have tax advantages) to cover the costs of annual healthcare expenses. And if you're one of the lucky few who are offered other perks, I want you to take advantage of them. Participate in stock purchase programs. Use meal and transportation credits, tuition reimbursement, and gym membership discounts. These perks positively affect your financial health. Once again, use your benefits because they are part of your compensation. You maximize earnings by using them.

So what benefits are you using?

Use this table of employer benefits and perks to compare what's offered to what you're actually using. Then schedule a time to speak with your HR manager to learn about your total compensation at work.

Benefits and Perks'	Offered or Using
Paid time off (vacation, sick, other)	
401(k) employer match	
Health insurance (health, dental, vision)	
Health savings account/flexible spending account	
Group term life insurance	
Disability insurance	
Stocks (options, restricted units)	
Employee stock purchase program	
Tuition reimbursement	
Public transportation credit	

Benefits and Perks*	Offered or Using
Student loan payment program	
Wellness programs (gym, healthy habits, workshops)	
Childcare	
In-office perks (snacks, lunches)	
Telecommuting/flexible work schedule	
Employee assistance program	
Credit union	
Discounts (shopping portals, affinity discounts)	

*See Appendix for the Benefits and Perks Worksheet.

STEP 3: MAKING MORE AT YOUR CURRENT JOB

You deserve to get paid more. And I want you to make more money working the same number of hours.

While paid overtime can be helpful, it isn't a sustainable way of earning. Working too many hours will drain you. And you'll be too exhausted and mentally drained to work on building passive income. So the best option is to get paid more for the work you're already doing.

Let's begin with a thought experiment: Do you think you will ever make $1 million? Put down the book and take a few minutes to think about this.

What thoughts came to mind? Can you see yourself earning a million dollars?

You either think you can or you think it's impossible.

I used to dream about making a million dollars. You probably have too. But many people believe they'll never make a million dollars. It got me wondering, which led to researching and then calculating how someone can earn a million dollars. After filtering out get-rich-quick schemes and sketchy business ideas, I learned how many of us can earn a million dollars by simply working a job.

Hear me out: you *can* earn a million dollars in your lifetime. The table illustrates how it can happen.

CAN YOU EARN $1,000,000 AT YOUR JOB?

Income from a job can add up to earning a million dollars in 10, 20, or 30 years.

	$30,000	$60,000	$90,000
10 Years	$395,000	$790,800	$1,186,300
20 Years	$1,103,600	$2,207,100	$3,310,700
30 Years	$2,371,700	$4,743,500	$7,115,200

It's not surprising that the more you make, the faster it is to make $1 million in earnings over your lifetime. This table factors a 6% annual salary increase. It can be a merit base increase from the same company or a salary increase from a new job.

There were three lessons I learned from the research. First, earning a million in your lifetime doesn't mean you'll see that amount hit your bank account. A percentage of earnings goes towards taxes, contributions, and so on. Second, getting paid more is crucial to reaching million-dollar earnings sooner. You simply need to earn more in the job you're doing. And lastly, earning a million dollars isn't the same as growing your net worth to a million dollars. There are people who make six-figure salaries and are not on track to having a million-dollar net worth. Turning earnings into income-generating assets is the key to financial independence. You'll learn how to do just that in the Grow Money pillar.

Why is it important to know that you can earn one million dollars? Because it will shift your mindset: you are or will be a million-dollar earner. Think about that for a moment. It's a powerful feeling to know how reachable it can be. Okay, it might take a lifetime to achieve, but knowing it can happen might motivate you to make it happen sooner.

The knowledge that your future self is a million-dollar earner should be motivational. It should inspire you. It should build confidence. All of this is important for what I need you to do next: asking for and getting your much-deserved pay raise.

YOUR EARNINGS AS RECORDED BY THE SOCIAL SECURITY ADMINISTRATION

Do you keep track of your earnings from previous years? If not, you're in luck because the Social Security Administration keeps a database of your earnings tracked by your Social Security number.

The Social Security Statement shows your record of all earnings received during your work history. It's available to everyone 25 years and over. The SSA keeps it to determine your eligibility for Social Security benefits upon retirement or disability.

Knowing the income you've earned in the past helps you understand how your earnings potential has grown or stalled. It's an eye-opening experience.

To get your SSA statement, visit ssa.gov.

Review the records to verify that your earning years are reflected correctly. Errors are possible, so look closely. You can verify the information by comparing it to your income tax filings.

Verify the following information:

- The Social Security number noted on your earnings statement is correct.
- The earned income amounts listed on the agency's records match your records of earnings as listed on your income tax forms.

If you find any errors, contact the Social Security Administration to have them corrected.

How much have you earned?

	Amount	Years	
Social Security Statement Reported Total Earnings	$		What are your earning years? Ex. 2005 – 2020 = 15 years

How to Get Your Much-Deserved Pay Raise

Asking for more money is a nerve-wracking experience, so some are inclined to avoid it. But you're not like the others. You know that pay raise is long overdue and you're ready to ask for it. Because I've been on opposite sides of the request, I've learned ways that have helped me and others increase their pay. They include the following eight steps.

Step 1: Start with a Question: "Do I Deserve A Pay Raise?"

Your answer must be a resounding "yes." The goal, however, is to get your boss to say "yes" enthusiastically.

Answering the first question leads to another important follow-up; "Why do you deserve a raise?" This question is about getting you to know your worth. It's about uncovering the reasons why a raise is long overdue. You want to answer the second question with facts, examples, and specific details. Know how your work contributes to department goals and overall company profitability. A well-prepared request can help your manager defend your pay raise with their bosses.

Step 2: Read Your Current Job Description

You must know the current requirements and scope of your job. Most employees haven't looked at their job descriptions since they were hired. The work requirements of the job have likely changed, but you were grandfathered into the old job description with the previous salary range.

Often, newer employees earn more with the same job title because the position encompasses more responsibilities or requires new skills. The increased requirements might have factored into higher starting salaries. Review the job descriptions: you might learn that you qualify for a promotion (let's say from analyst I to analyst II), which comes with a salary increase.

Step 3: Get Reliable Salary Data

Know the salary ranges for your position at your employer. If you're on the lower part of your position's salary range, you have a bit of room to negotiate. Some companies are transparent when it comes to salary ranges. Do your research.

It's also vital to get salary data from outside your company to determine the average rate for similar jobs. Now, you'll need to adjust data to reflect the industry, company size, employees, annual revenues, and location. Use the results as a benchmark to request a pay raise. However, I want you to also know salaries go beyond your manager and must be approved by human resources as well. Most HR departments have done the work to ensure they are offering competitive salaries but that isn't always the case. Go to salary.com for wage comparisons.

Step 4: List All Your Accomplishments

Make it easier on yourself by using an online document or spreadsheet to track your accomplishments. Having a readily available list can assist you in clearly demonstrating why you merit a salary increase. It also enables you to quantify (e.g., reduced department overhead by 20%) and qualify (e.g., worked with senior leadership on a community service project) for the raise.

Write down your work highlights, projects, awards, and training you've received. Did your work increase revenues, reduce expenses, or innovate a process? Write them down. Were you given new tasks or an expanded role? Make sure it's on your list. Did you get a glowing email from your boss, coworker, or client? Include the praise in the document. And while you're at it, add the most significant accomplishments in your resume and LinkedIn profile.

Step 5: Choose the Right Time

Timing is important. I want you to consider these two things:

- **Ask for a raise when your manager's thoughts aren't preoccupied with time-sensitive deliverables.** Be mindful of monthly, quarterly, and annual deadlines. You want your manager's attention when no major agendas compete for their time. So avoid asking a few days before your boss goes on vacation or during the holidays. This increases the attention they'll give to your request. And when you have salary data, an updated resume, and a list of accomplishments, it'll show you respect their time by being prepared for the discussion.

- **Ask for a pay raise when you're at your best.** Don't ask for a raise when your work performance has been less than stellar. Negotiating a raise is harder when you have difficulty coming to work on time, completing projects, or meeting deadlines. Before discussing the pay raise with your boss, create a plan to improve your performance.

Step 6: Know Your Employer's Financials

Before asking, understand your department's budget and your company's financial standing. Is it profitable or in the red? Is your department achieving its goals? If your company is going through layoffs or reporting losses, it's not the time to ask for a raise. On the other hand, a profitable company or a high-performing department can have additional resources to increase pay for top performers.

Step 7: Schedule the Appointment

I recommend setting a separate meeting to discuss salary. Don't try to squeeze in the conversation during project status meetings. If you have monthly one-on-ones, choose a month where you'll have more time. You want their undivided attention and enough time to discuss your salary goals. Give them a heads-up and follow up with a calendar appointment to speak with them. I want you to immediately set up the meeting to discuss the raise. Don't let weeks and months pass.

Before requesting the meeting, make sure you've done the previous steps in this section.

Step 8: Avoid These Pitfalls

When you have your meeting, focus on your contributions and how your performance impacts the department. Avoid doing these two things:

- **Don't compare yourself to coworkers.** When discussing your raise with your manager, avoid mentioning what your colleagues earn or how they perform. They already know how much your coworkers are making. The focus should be solely on your accomplishments and contributions to the company.

- **Keep personal financial issues separate.** Discussing financial challenges in the context of a pay raise request detracts from your professional achievements. Managers may empathize, but it won't be a decisive factor in getting a raise. Instead, high-light your work performance and how you add value to the organization.

WHAT HAPPENS IF YOU'RE DENIED A PAY RAISE?

I've been denied pay raise before. It always felt like a slap in the face. There were different reasons given, none of which I even remember. But I did have a positive takeaway from all the "nos" I received. I focused my time and energy on developing my career. I no longer wanted to be just the best worker in the company. I wanted to be the sought-after expert in my profession.

If you're denied a pay increase, do the following:

Continue to update your achievements. Whether or not you receive the raise this time, maintain an ongoing record of your accomplishments. The list will be helpful in future discussions and evaluations with your manager. It's also useful when you apply for a position in a different department or company.

Enhance your skills and network. Take advantage of workshops and cross-departmental projects to improve your skill set and expand your network within the company. I've found that participating in community outreach initia-tives can help you build connections with the leadership team. They are often the ones who lead them. And attending professional conferences is a great way to meet managers with future job openings.

Stay positive. If your employer can't meet your salary expectations, avoid letting it affect your performance or attitude. You may have another opportunity to ask and get the raise in a few months. If you're feeling frustrated, channel that emotion into creating a plan to leave your job in good standing. Keeping optimistic is good for your financial and mental health.

TAKE ACTION

Use the worksheets in the Appendix to help you complete the exercises.

1. Learn the details of your paycheck and review your pay stub.
2. Access your Social Security Statement by visiting SSA.gov.
3. Review the Get Your Pay Raise Checklist.

Optimize Your Paycheck Recap

In this chapter, you learned the three specific ways to optimize your earnings:

- **Step 1:** Improving your net pay through deductions and contributions
- **Step 2:** Maximizing your earnings using employer benefits
- **Step 3:** Making more at your current job

To summarize, you learned to optimize your paycheck by using strategies such as adjusting tax withholdings, utilizing deductions, and increasing contributions. You gained a better understanding of your benefits and perks that support your financial health. And you were given tips to get that much-deserved pay raise. These lessons taught you how to earn more with your current job without having to work more hours.

Congrats! You've learned the steps to optimize your earnings and are on your way to taking full advantage of your employee benefits package. In the next chapter, you'll learn how to multiply your income streams.

CHAPTER 5

Multiply Your Income Streams

L et income flow into your life.

A few years ago, I was flying over the American Southwest on my way to San Diego, California. I was in awe of the Colorado River as it cut through the Grand Canyon. The sheer volume of water and energy was mesmerizing. Then I remembered that the Colorado River starts out as a small stream in the Rocky Mountains. The tributaries and streams that flow into the Colorado make up the river.

Think of income as a river. The river exists because of its sources, such as tributaries and streams. The more tributaries and streams, the stronger and bigger the river. You want to have a strong-flowing income river.

For example, having a nine-to-five job is an income source. Having a full-time job and a part-time job means you have two income streams. This can help with your finances but drain you of your time. Whereas if you had a job, self-published a book on Amazon, and owned rental property, you'd have multiple and diversified income streams for greater peace of mind.

It took me a long time to figure out the income strategy that allows me to live my life on my terms. I spent a lot of time in exhausting ventures that didn't create sustainable income. But now I know better, and I earn better.

In this lesson, I will share exactly how you can earn more and work less. You'll learn that the five in the 3-5-7 PRIME method refers to the five passive income ideas. The steps in this chapter are:

■ **Step 1:** Understanding your income number
■ **Step 2:** Identifying your active income opportunities
■ **Step 3:** Finding your passive income streams
■ **Step 4:** Starting a side hustle

Let's get multiplying!

STEP 1: UNDERSTANDING YOUR INCOME NUMBER

How many income types do you have?

You might have one, or maybe two. And that's okay; you're just starting out. But I challenge you to go beyond your income starting point. I want you to have multiple income streams, too.

So what is your income number? Below is an example of how to calculate your income number.

Income Number			
Income	Gross Monthly Amount	Gross Annual Amount	Type (*active, passive, portfolio*)
Smile Corp	$3,500	$42,000	active
Freelance work	$1,500	$18,000	active
Renting room	$500	$6,000	passive
YouTube earnings	$100	$1,200	active/passive
Savings interest	$25	$300	portfolio
Etsy shop printables	$200	$2,400	passive
Total	**$5,825**	**$69,900**	**6**
Income Number (Total of Income Types)			

What incomes do you have, how much is flowing in, and what type are they?

As you think about your income strategy, it might be easier to start with active income because it requires less capital to start. Eventually, you're tasked to shift your focus to passive income sources, including portfolio income. But first, let's define the three income types: active, passive, and portfolio.

Active income is from any service- or performance-based activity. This includes money from a job, tips, commissions, and bonuses. In contrast, **passive income** is received from limited activity; it doesn't require daily and active participation to generate income. **Portfolio income**, a subcategory of passive income, comes from interests, dividends, and capital gains. For tax purposes, it's essential to distinguish between these income types. because they're treated differently by the IRS.

Active Income	Passive Income	Portfolio Income
▪ Your full-time job	▪ Rental property	▪ Interest from savings, certificates, etc.
▪ Part-time work	▪ Royalties from book	▪ Interest paid from lending money
▪ Driving others	▪ Licensing artwork	▪ Dividends
▪ Delivering packages	▪ Online shop	▪ Capital gains
▪ Content creating	▪ Blogs	
▪ Babysitting	▪ Business profits	
▪ Completing surveys		

The great news is that you can have various income types flowing in. And the choice is yours to make.

STEP 2: IDENTIFYING YOUR ACTIVE INCOME OPPORTUNITIES

We earn money by either exchanging our time or investing our money. If you don't have money to invest, exchange your time instead. Adding active income streams is the way to go when starting the journey to multiply your income. There are two active income types:

1. **Active income from employment:** The money you make working for a company or someone else where you get a paycheck and taxes are taken out

2. **Active income from self-employment:** The earnings you make working for yourself through your own business, freelance endeavors, or occasional side gigs

The table shows a list of active income ideas.

Traditional full-time and part-time work Many companies offer additional perks along with wages.	**Having a blog** Write about your passions and interests that help others too.
Freelance writing Write for blogs, business websites, and other outlets.	**Tasking** Complete tasks for others in their homes or workplaces.
Resume writing Help job seekers by crafting their best resume.	**Selling used items** Sell used goods (clothes, furniture, tools) through online marketplaces.
Virtual assisting Provide administrative support, such as answering emails and scheduling meetings.	**Tutoring** Share your knowledge by tutoring students of all ages.
Graphic designing Design logos, websites, advertisements, brochures, flyers, posters, etc.	**Short-term rentals** Rent your bedroom, garage, driveway, land, tech gadgets, camera equipment, and more.
Driving around Deliver packages and groceries, and drive people to their destinations.	**Selling handmade and custom crafts** Offer hand lettering, knitting, woodwork, and downloadable prints.
Editing Videos and podcast editing, and PowerPoint proofreading.	**Helping others** Cleaning homes, babysitting, assisting the elderly, and pet sitting or dog walking.
For an updated list of active income ideas, visit thesmilemoney.com/book.	

There is absolutely nothing wrong with active income.

Just be mindful not to fall into the time-for-pay trap. Let's say you took a part-time retail job in addition to your full-time employment. You now have two income streams. The additional money is great but all your time is spent working. And even if you wanted to work more hours, there are only so many hours in a day. You can see how exchanging your time for a paycheck (active income) limits your earning potential.

As I shared earlier, my speaking and consulting gigs are strong income sources in which I am actively involved. However, as I progressed in my income strategy, I wanted less reliance on active income sources. I shifted from active income work to passive income streams.

Active income is truly about the hustle and grind. You can hustle for a reason and grind for season. But I want you to do it with purpose. Make as much as possible through your active income sources, then funnel that money into passive income streams. Once you do, you are entering a whole new level of earning.

STEP 3: FINDING YOUR PASSIVE INCOME STREAMS

Passive income is earned without having to actively work for it or without having to exchange time for money. Again, the five in the 3-5-7 PRIME method refers to the five passive income ideas you'll read in this step.

1. Passive Income Ideas Involving the Stock Market

You'll learn more about how to invest in the Grow Money pillar. For now, here are three ways to earn passively with shares.

■ **Dividend-paying stocks**

Start investing in stocks that pay dividends—profits that companies pay out to shareholders in cash or stock. Dividends are usually paid at the end of each quarter and are considered good investments because they provide regular income for investors.

■ **Index funds and exchange-traded funds (ETFs)**

Instead of purchasing individual stocks, you can buy funds that hold dividend-paying stocks. With index funds, you get a basket of companies that mirror the performance of a specific index, such as the S&P 500.

■ **Interest income from bonds**

Lend money to corporations or the government using bonds. This investment is considered a lower risk, and your returns are generally lower. For example, a government bond may give you a 5% annual return compared to an index fund that could return 10% during the same period.

2. Passive Income Ideas Involving Banks or Credit Unions

Use interest-earning accounts offered at local and online financial institutions.

■ **High-yield savings accounts**

Save your money in a high-yield savings account (HYSA) to grow your money faster. Interest rates in high-yield savings accounts are often much higher than the national average. For example, you can get a 1% interest rate with an HYSA compared to 0.10% through a big bank. You can find HYSAs offered by online banks or credit unions.

■ **Certificates (CDs)**

Generally, certificates of deposit earn a higher rate than regular savings accounts. Using certificates helps you earn more interest on your money.

3. Passive Income Ideas Involving Real Estate

Investments in real estate often come with active landlord responsibilities. The following is how you can passively earn with real estate.

■ **Rental property**

Owning property for rental income is a reliable long-term strategy. However, they often come with stressors like unruly tenants and high maintenance costs. You can reduce active participation by hiring a property management company to do the work, from leasing to maintenance to cleaning.

- **Short-term rentals**

  Instead of leasing your rental properties to tenants, you can offer them as short-stay rentals through Airbnb. Or if you have an extra bedroom, backyard, driveway, parking spot, garage, or basement, there are services you can use to rent out the space. Renting out space requires your activity, but it turns underused spaces into income earners.

- **Real Estate Investment Trust**

  This belongs to "investing in the stock market," but you can consider this a passive income idea involving real estate. REITs own income-producing properties like shopping centers, office buildings, hotels, apartment complexes, and industrial parks. They are publicly traded corporations with shares that can appreciate in value and pay dividends.

4. Passive Income Ideas Involving Businesses

- **Peer-to-peer investing**

  Invest in personal or business loans through peer-to-peer lending companies. They match investors to borrowers through a proprietary platform and pool investments to fund loans. You earn interest as the borrower makes monthly payments.

- **Silent business partner**

  Instead of running a business, you can invest in companies and earn passive income through business profits. If you have significant assets or are considered a high-net-worth person and accredited investor, you may have the opportunity to invest in private equity funds. But you can also consider investing in a family or friend's business venture with an agreement on a profit share.

5. Semi-Passive Income Options

The following can be considered passive after considerable time and work effort. I like to think of them as semi-passive income.

▪ **Blogging**

A good way to build passive income is to start a blog. As your traffic grows, you can earn income in multiple ways from advertisements, affiliate links, sponsored posts, and your own digital products. It does take time to grow an audience, but once you find your niche topic, the amount of time you spend may be significantly reduced. It can be a solid source of income for years, especially through affiliate marketing.

▪ **Licensing**

If you enjoy taking photos and videos, consider licensing your images for use by others. Many entrepreneurs and businesses pay to use creative works. Your creations can become a residual income source for years to come.

▪ **Publishing**

Turn your words into a book and self-publish on Amazon, Barnes & Noble, and more. After your upfront investment in time, your published books can turn into reliable sources of extra income.

▪ **YouTubing**

This isn't really passive because you have to film, edit, and publish videos consistently. However, once your videos are published, they can continuously earn money with unlimited income potential. You'll earn money through ads that play on your channel, from affiliate links, or by allowing viewers to buy physical products.

As you can see from this list, some upfront investment is often required with any passive income opportunity. You must have either the time or the money. If you don't have extra cash to invest, use your time to maximize your active income sources first. Maximize the amount of money you can generate through activity and use the earnings to aggressively invest in passive income streams.

For an updated list of active and passive income ideas, visit thesmilemoney.com/book.

STEP 4: STARTING A SIDE HUSTLE

When thinking about side hustles, consider if you're looking to make extra cash or looking for a different path in life. You certainly can do both. Knowing this can help you strategize for better outcomes.

In his bestseller, *Side Hustles: From Idea to Income in 27 Days*, Chris Guillebeau writes about the importance of having a side hustle in addition to your day job. He defines a side hustle as a skill or an interest turned into an income-generating business. His definition of side hustles is similar to how I define passive income. You must devote some time to the hustle, but you're not limited in money made based on active participation.

Alternatively, David Carlson, an online friend and author of *Hustle Away Debt*, wrote about using side hustles to eliminate debt. His approach often shows how active side hustles can help achieve financial goals sooner. In his book, he shares dozens of side hustle ideas that helped him and others achieve their goals. Interestingly enough, some active side hustles can turn into passive income streams.

The Entrepreneurial Dream

I am not against corporate jobs. In fact, working a traditional job comes with a steady salary and benefits, which is not the case with self-employment. The reality is that entrepreneurs work more hours for little pay (especially in the early years) compared to working for an employer. And if you can't afford your basic living expenses, you'll be too stressed to build your business.

My advice to budding entrepreneurs: you don't have to quit your job to start a side hustle or to explore a business idea. Think of your employer as the first investor. Allocate some of your salary to building your company. Once your business income is equivalent to your corporate salary, you can say goodbye to your job.

I do have a word of caution: be wary of the promises made in YouTube ads or by influencers on Instagram and TikTok. Online marketers will hype the idea of becoming your own boss and becoming rich from it.

Understand that they make their income when you buy their get-rich-quick systems. Here's their secret: the key to their success is taking your hard-earned money by selling the dream.

There are no quick ways to earn lots of money ethically. It takes time and effort.

So do your homework. There are valuable systems and courses available offered by real experts with a wealth of experience. I do pay for courses and expert advice because they are shortcuts to help me do things more efficiently and save time.

To summarize my experience and advice I've learned from experts and books:

1. Find a side hustle you would enjoy doing.
2. Devote time to being the best at it.
3. Use free tools to support your efforts.
4. Pay for systems that make work more efficient.
5. Determine if income can replace your full-time salary.
6. Make it a sustainable income-generating business.
7. Remain persistent.
8. Evaluate your time investment based on revenues, personal income, and happiness.

Now, what kind of side hustles can you do? Answer the questions in this chart to get your ideas flowing.

Side hustle idea questions:	Ideas
What stuff can you sell?	
What service can you offer?	
Do you have a driver's license and a car?	
Do you have unused space and enjoy hosting?	
Are you a skilled wordsmith, artist, photographer, or graphic designer?	

WHY DO YOU NEED MORE THAN ONE INCOME?

There are several reasons why you should multiply and diversify your income, such as:

1. Surviving unemployment

There's no such thing as true job security. Your company may do well today, but things can change in the next month or years. And if you lose your job, money from unemployment benefits may not provide enough cash to cover your monthly expenses.

2. Ability to make ends meet

Even if you work hard and keep your life simple, your income may not keep up with inflation and the higher cost of living. Having multiple income streams can stop this vicious cycle. With more cash each month, it'll be easier to cover your monthly expenses and reduce some of your financial worries.

3. Building your savings

Income from your day job can pay for everyday expenses, such as housing, transportation, and utilities. Your second stream can help you reach your savings goals.

4. Paying off debt

Don't get stuck in a minimum payment trap. Extra money can go towards your debt.

5. Finding a new career

As you slowly increase the income earned from your secondary income stream, you can quit your full-time job and earn a living doing what you love.

6. Reaching financial independence

With multiple incomes, you can increase investments to hit your financial independence number sooner. You'll learn more about this in the Grow Money pillar.

TAKE ACTION

Use the worksheets in the Appendix to implement the ideas.

1. Calculate your income number.
2. Complete the side hustle exercise.

Multiply Your Income Streams Recap

This chapter explored two primary types of income: active and passive. Active income is earned through service or performance-based activities like jobs, tips, commissions, and bonuses. In contrast, passive income requires limited ongoing effort and includes portfolio income, like interests, dividends, and capital gains.

The lessons explained these steps:

- **Step 1:** Understanding your income number
- **Step 2:** Identifying your active income opportunities
- **Step 3:** Finding your passive income streams
- **Step 4:** Starting a side hustle

Remember, the strategic approach to active income: hustle for a reason and a season. Maximize your active income sources to build your passive income streams.

Congratulations! You've mastered the steps to multiply your income. In the next chapter, you'll learn how to diversify your income sources.

CHAPTER **6**

Diversify Your
Income Sources

One of my friends has always been good with her finances. She had a steady job, earned a decent income, and even managed to save a portion of it. Yet deep down, she felt a sense of unease. My friend reached out to me because she wanted to secure her financial future.

I asked her to complete an income checkup and she had a realization. Her income covered her needs and some wants, but it was clear that relying solely on one source didn't provide the peace of mind she sought. My friend's story is not unique. It mirrors the reality of so many who depend on one income for their financial security: it's much harder to achieve.

I've learned that a key to financial well-being is diversifying income sources. My advice to my friend was to do just that. And it's my recommendation you do the same. In this chapter, you'll learn that the seven in the 3-5-7 PRIME method refers to the seven sources of income. The lessons explain the following steps:

- **Step 1:** Understanding your seven available sources of income

- **Step 2:** Assessing your income sources

- **Step 3:** Creating your income strategy

STEP 1: UNDERSTANDING YOUR SEVEN AVAILABLE SOURCES OF INCOME

You've learned about active, passive, and portfolio income and grasped the importance of having multiple income streams. Now it's time to diversify the sources for greater flexibility and peace of mind. Knowing the seven income sources will play a critical role in shaping your income strategy.

Earned Income

Your regular paycheck and the money you make by trading your time is called earned income. It's the money you earn whenever you put in your time, energy, or skills for a paycheck. Many folks depend on earned income as their primary source, whether it's a steady salary or wages per hour. However, it's essential to realize that the amount you can earn is limited by the hours you can put in.

Rental Income

When someone rents from you, they pay you money for using the property. It could be a house, an apartment, or even a room. The best part is that rental income requires less daily activity to earn this money. Many financially independent people I've spoken with have said that rental income was their path to financial freedom.

Profit Income

You can own a business without having to run the day-to-day operations or be involved in the decision-making. Instead, you invest money in the business to get a piece of the profits. Profits are what's left over after expenses are deducted from the revenues generated. Your share of the profit is based on your ownership percentage. Now, there may be instances when you can make earned and profit income. For instance, a business you own pays you a salary and distributes profits once a year.

Royalty Income

Being a creator, I love this source. Imagine earning money through licensing your work: books, music, artwork, or any of your creations. It's a fulfilling way to generate passive income while sharing your creativity with the world.

The next three sources belong to the portfolio income category, offering unique opportunities for investment and growth.

Interest Income

When you lend or save money, you get paid with interest. It's the fee you earn for letting others—banks, credit unions, governments, or other financial institutions—borrow your money for a period of time. The best part is that you don't have to work extra to earn this income. It works for you and grows over time.

Dividend Income

Publicly traded companies pay their shareholders dividends as a share of profits. It's a passive way to generate a steady income. You can earn dividends by investing in stocks, exchange-traded funds (ETFs), and index funds with history and consistency in paying dividends to shareholders.

Capital Gains

Capital gains come from selling assets that have grown in value over time. This can be real estate, stocks, or other valuable items. Capital gains are the difference between the original purchase price and the selling price of assets. Suppose you bought your house five years ago for $250,000 and sold it for $350,000. You would realize a capital gain of $100,000.

Now that you have grasped the seven income sources, it's time to assess where you stand.

STEP 2: ASSESSING YOUR INCOME SOURCES

Refer to the seven sources of income. How diversified are you? How many income sources do you currently have? Complete the checkup here.

Income Sources Checkup		
Sources	Description	Do you have any?
Earned Income	Money earned from exchanging your time	Yes / No
Profit Income	Money earned from business profits	Yes / No
Rental Income	Money earned from rental properties	Yes / No
Royalty Income	Money earned from licensing creations	Yes / No
Interest Income	Money earned from lending to others	Yes / No
Dividend Income	Money earned from stocks and funds	Yes / No
Capital Gains	Money earned from selling assets	Yes / No

STEP 3: CREATING YOUR INCOME STRATEGY

Did you know that financially independent people have multiple sources of income? They don't rely on just one source. In fact, most millionaires have five or more income streams coming in. How many do you have? Let's create your income strategy!

1. **Start by listing all the income you currently have.** This could include your salary, side hustles, rental income, or investments.

2. **Identify any gaps or opportunities where you can increase your income.** Are there any skills you have that you can monetize? Can you explore new ways to earn money on the side?

3. **Think about how you can multiply your income.** Are there ways to scale up your current ventures or investments? Can you find additional streams of income that complement your existing ones?

4. **Diversify your income.** Look for different sources that can provide stability and reduce risk. Consider passive income options like investments or royalties.

When creating your income strategy, it's important to understand how taxes affect different incomes. Yaroslav Tashak, the accounting expert behind CPA-gurus.com, shared the following:

> Active income, like wages, is taxed at ordinary income tax rates and incurs FICA taxes [the mandatory payroll taxes for Social Security and Medicare that are withheld from your paycheck]. On the other hand, passive income sources, including interest, dividends, and real estate income, aren't subject to FICA taxes.
>
> While it might seem tempting to focus on passive income due to its tax advantages, I believe it's essential first to maximize active income. Once a stable active income is established, one can strategically diversify into passive income streams.

The IRS tax rates can differ significantly depending on the type of income made. But don't let this discourage you from diversifying your sources. Consider seeking guidance from a tax professional for your specific situation.

Remember, building a strong income strategy takes time and effort but is well worth it.

Income Strategy Example*			
Income List	Source (active, passive, portfolio)	Stream Type (earned, rental, profit, royalty, interest, dividend, capital gains)	Existing or Planned (current or planned for the future)
Smile Corp, full-time	Active	Earned Income	Existing
Freelancing writing	Active	Earned Income	Existing
Uber	Active	Earned Income	Existing
Esty store	Passive	Profit Income	Planned
Rental property	Passive	Rental Income	Existing
Amazon book	Passive	Royalty Income	Planned

Income Strategy Example*			
Income List	**Source** (active, passive, portfolio)	**Stream Type** (earned, rental, profit, royalty, interest, dividend, capital gains)	**Existing or Planned** (current or planned for the future)
Savings account	Portfolio	Interest Income	Existing
Stocks sold	Portfolio	Capital Gains	Planned
AT&T quarterly dividends	Portfolio	Dividend Income	Existing

See Appendix for the Income Strategy Worksheet.

TAKE ACTION

1. Use the income strategy worksheet in the Appendix to identify active and passive income opportunities.

 Diversify Your Income Sources Recap

In this chapter, you learned a key to financial well-being is income diversification and you now know the seven sources of income: earned, rental, profit, royalty, interest, dividend, and capital gains. The steps in the lesson were:

- **Step 1:** Understanding your seven available sources of income
- **Step 2:** Assessing your income sources
- **Step 3:** Creating your income strategy

You've now taken the crucial steps towards securing your financial future.

EARN MONEY SUMMARY

A celebration is in order! You now have the skills to optimize, maximize, multiply, and diversify your income. In the Earn Money pillar, you learned the 3-5-7 PRIME method. You grasped how to make as much as possible through active streams and discovered the ways to invest those earnings into passive income-generating sources. The pillar presented these lessons:

- **Lesson 1:** Optimize Your Paycheck (3)
- **Lesson 2:** Multiply Your Income Streams (5)
- **Lesson 3:** Diversify Your Income Sources (7)

Remember, making your money smile is about less time working to earn a living and more time living off your earnings.

In the next chapter, you'll start the Grow Money pillar to help you grow your money through investing. The pillar focuses on building your savings, contributing to retirement, and investing for financial independence.

PILLAR III

Grow Money

Investing Strategy

Do you have savings accounts tucked away? Are you contributing to a 401(k)? Have you ventured into the world of IRAs? Do you have money in the stock market? Are you an investor?

If these questions get you tense, take a slow, deep breath. I don't want you to be stressed. Many of us start with nothing and work our way up to something.

Start making money with money.

I want you to know that investing is for everyone. Investing is for you. And it's entirely possible you're already investing too. If you're saving money in an account earning interest, you're investing. If you're contributing to an employer-sponsored retirement plan like a 401(k) plan, you're investing. You see, you've been an investor all along.

The third pillar is Grow Money—the investing strategy—to increase wealth. Make your money smile by giving it a job. So give your paycheck, earnings, and the cash stashed in your drawer a purpose through investments.

| Grow Money | Put your money to work so it earns for you. |

In this pillar, you'll learn how money grows, ways to maximize returns on savings accounts, how to plan your retirement money, and ways to start the path to financial independence. It features the following:

- **Lesson 1:** Build Your Investments
- **Lesson 2:** Contribute to Your Retirement
- **Lesson 3:** Invest for Independence

After these chapters, you'll be an intentional investor building wealth.

Let's get growing.

7

Build Your Investments

totally understand why investing can seem intimidating. I was intimidated myself. It seemed too complex with the charts and over-whelming with the news. My fear ended when I shifted into an investor mindset. I invest to build sustainable wealth, not to use get-rich-quick schemes. This mindset has minimized my mistakes and got me to start making money.

You see, mindset plays a pivotal role in investing. How you think about investing can greatly influence whether you take the first steps or remain hesitant. But the longer you put it off, the less time you'll have money working for you.

SHIFT YOUR MINDSET TO GROW YOUR MONEY

Start early. But it's never too late to begin. The sooner you start saving and invest-ing money, the more you'll benefit from the power of compounding.

Start small. Something is better than nothing. Start with any amount you can reasonably do. You can increase your investments as your earnings grow.

(Continued)

(*Continued*)

Be consistent. Use automation to stay on schedule regardless of market conditions. You'll benefit from dollar-cost averaging without stressing yourself trying to keep up with daily market conditions.

Think long-term. Keep your eye on the prize and understand that investments can take time to grow. Patience and strategy builds wealth.

Don't speculate. Unless you plan to learn how to do trades and research stock, stick with the simplicity of index funds and ETFs. As you meet your goals and grow your money, there may be future opportunities to buy and sell individual stocks.

Don't be greedy. Be mindful of how greed plays a role in investing decisions. The desire to make quick money in the stock market can be tempting but foolhardy. Understand your tolerance for risk and think long-term.

As you continue to read along, you'll understand how to make money work for you. In this chapter, you'll learn these steps:

- **Step 1:** Getting started with investing
- **Step 2:** Compounding your returns
- **Step 3:** Earning more on savings

STEP 1: GETTING STARTED WITH INVESTING: THE IMPACT OF TIME

Don't wait until the "perfect" time. The perfect time is right now!

"You simply have to start because wealth is made through investing," advises Kevin Matthews II, a friend I've known for many years and someone who makes investing simple.

Kevin founded buildingbread.com, an investment education company empowering others to create generational wealth through investing. He's a former financial advisor who managed a $140 million portfolio during his advisory career.

"You can use money to buy back time," says Kevin, "and you can use the time to make more money."

When you think about growing money, consider how time impacts that growth. Here is an example using my twin nieces, Clementine and Matilda. Let's say they both started working right after college. Clementine started investing immediately at 22 years old. However, Matilda started 10 years later and began investing at 32. At 67 years old, Clementine's investment would be worth twice as much as Matilda's because of the power of compound interest, which allows money to grow over time.

HOW STARTING EARLIER MATTERS

More time allows your money to grow even more. The chart illustrates the following:

- The difference 10 years can make in growing money.
- $5,000 was the amount invested each year until reaching 67 years old.
- 7% was the average annual rate of return.

Clementine, who started 10 years earlier, will retire with $900,000 more than Matilda. Clementine's early start and additional $50,000 (10 years x $5,000) contribution have reaped the benefits of time and compounding.

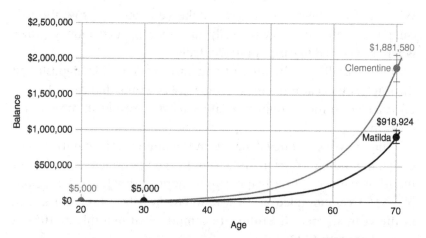

Note: Earning 7% interest on a savings account is highly unlikely. As of this writing, the savings rates range from 0% to 4% with online banks. However, the example holds true in how compounding works.
This example is for illustrative purposes only, assuming a moderate 7% return rate on your stock market investments. The historic annualized average return of the S&P 500 is around 10.5% since its inception in 1957.
Source: Adapted from https://www.spglobal.com/.

I want you to understand that starting later is much better than never starting. In the example, Matilda *can* choose to retire a decade later at 77, allowing her investments to grow an additional 10 years. So all is not lost. It would just require waiting a bit longer.

Again, the earlier you start investing, the less money you need and the more time it has to grow. But if you start late, you can still benefit from time by investing for a few more years. The key message here is this: don't wait, and just start.

STEP 2: COMPOUNDING YOUR RETURNS

Grow your money through the power of compounding.

During my conversation with Kevin, he explained that time affects wealth creation through compounding. So the earlier you start investing, the less you'll need to contribute because of the power of time and compound interest.

What Is Compounding?

Whenever you hear experts say, "Make your money grow through compound interest," they're really just sharing how money grows when it's allowed to earn uninterruptedly.

Compounding is the interest you earn on the initial deposit and the interest you continue to accumulate. Each time that earned interest is added to the account, the larger balance results in more interest earned.

The growth of money depends on the interest rate and frequency of compounding. Your money can be compounded annually or monthly, with the latter helping your money grow faster. For example, $100 compounded at 10% annually will be $110 by the end of the year, whereas if $100 were compounded monthly at 10%, it would be worth $111.

Here's an example and table to illustrate the concept of compounding annually. On January 1, Alex opened a savings account that offered a 5% interest rate. His initial deposit was $100. How much will he have in four years?

Year	Starting Principal	Interest Earned	Ending Balance
1	$100 (initial)	$5	$105
2	$105	$5.25	$110.25
3	$110.25	$5.51	$115.76
4	$115.76	$5.78	$121.54

As you can see, the amount of interest earned increases yearly as the principal balance increases. This is the power of compound interest!

The good news is that there are other things you can do to grow your money. You can increase the savings amount, extend the time, or use an account that offers a higher interest rate. Doing one or all of these things will compound your money even more.

When it comes to your money, I want you to ask yourself these questions: How much will your money grow through compounding if you start with a larger balance? How much would it grow if you continue to make deposits? How much more will you earn with a higher interest rate? How much larger will the balance grow by investing longer?

Again there are things you can do to make compounding work for you.

How Does Compounding Work with Stock Investments?

The previous example you've read focused on the money in a savings account. Your investments in the stock market work similarly. Time continues to play a role, along with the growth in the value of the stock.

First, it's essential to know that when you invest in stocks, you become a part-owner of a company. As an investor, your returns come from two main sources:

- **Capital Appreciation:** If the stock's value increases over time, you can sell it at a higher price and make a profit.
- **Dividends:** Some companies share their profits with shareholders by paying dividends. It's like receiving a small portion of the company's earnings as a reward for being a shareholder.

Second, here's where compounding comes into play. When you reinvest the returns from your investments, you begin to earn with your original investment and on the reinvested returns. This process of earning returns on returns is called compound growth: a powerful concept in investing because it allows your investments to grow exponentially over time.

Finally, here's something else I want you to know. If you haven't invested for at least 10 years, then you haven't seen the real benefits of compound growth. You build wealth by staying invested for the long term.

COMPOUND GROWTH OF INVESTMENTS

Time is your best friend when it comes to capitalizing on the interest earned on your money. The longer your money is invested, the more it can grow. Time works in your favor, emphasizing the importance of starting early or extending your investment period.

To illustrate, here's an example of how much $100 will grow over time and in what year the interest earned will surpass the principal contributions made.

- Initial deposit: $100
- Monthly contributions: $100
- Average rate of return: 7%

Compounding works in your favor the longer you're invested. In this example, the interest earned will surpass principal contributions in year 20. So you've earned more than the amount you've saved. How amazing is that?

STEP 3: EARNING MORE ON SAVINGS

Use better accounts to turn your savings into a type of investment.

Your money grows through interest earned, like rent paid on your money. When you save money in an interest-bearing account, the bank pays you to keep your cash with them. The power of compounding is amplified by having money saved in an account offering a higher interest rate.

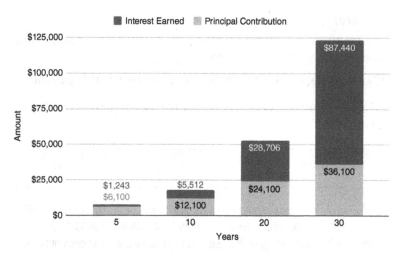

This example is for illustrative purposes only, assuming a moderate 7% return rate on your stock market investments. The historic annualized average return of the S&P 500 is around 10.5% since its inception in 1957. *Source:* Adapted from https://www.spglobal.com/.

You can keep your money in a traditional savings account, but they pay the least amount of interest. These other options allow you to earn more while keeping the risks low:

- **Option 1:** Using high-yield savings accounts (HYSAs)
- **Option 2:** Using CD laddering

Option 1: Using High-Yield Savings Accounts (HYSAs)

High-yield savings accounts (HYSAs) have higher interest rates than the national average. They are offered by online banks and some credit unions, which often have lower operational overhead than traditional banks. This allows them to offer higher interest rates on savings accounts. You can find HYSAs by visiting the financial marketplace on phroogal.com.

RULE OF 72: WHEN WILL YOUR MONEY DOUBLE?

The rule of 72 is a simple mathematical shortcut to estimate the time it takes for money to double in value at a given interest rate.

(Continued)

(*Continued*)

To use the rule of 72, divide the number 72 by the interest rate. The answer is the number of years it will take for your money to double.

72 / Annual Rate of Return = Number of Years for Amount to Double

For example, if you save money at a 6% interest rate, it will take about 12 years to double.

72	Divided	Annual Rate	Equals	Years
72	÷	6	=	12

The rule of 72 is a simple way to get a rough estimate, but it's not always accurate. The actual number of years it takes for money to double will depend on the exact interest rate, the consistency of that rate, and other factors, such as compounding.

Give it a try: How long will it take for your money to double? Check the current interest rate you're earning on a savings account.

72	Divided	Annual Rate	Equals	Years
72	÷		=	

Option 2: Using CD Laddering

Certificates of deposit (CDs) offer higher interest rates than standard savings accounts. The main difference is that your money is locked in for a set period of time or term. CD terms can range from 30 days to five years or more, with longer terms typically offering higher interest rates. However, if you withdraw your money early, you may be subject to a penalty, often equal to a few months of interest.

To grow your money while keeping access to some of your savings, use CD laddering. It involves dividing your money into specific amounts and depositing each amount into a CD with a different maturity date. This way, you will have access to some of your money every few months while still earning higher interest rates on the money that is still in the CDs.

For example, if you have $10,000 to invest, you could divide it into four equal amounts of $2,500 and deposit each amount into a CD with a one-year term, a two-year term, a three-year term, and a four-year term.

After one year, you would have access to the $2,500 invested in the one-year CD. You could then reinvest that money into a new one-year CD, or you could use it for other purposes. The other three CDs would continue to earn interest until their term ends.

CD laddering is a simple way to earn higher interest rates with lower risks while still having access to some of your money.

HOW CD LADDERS WORK

Let's say you have $20,000 saved in your Opportunity Fund to cover nine months of living expenses. You could use a CD ladder strategy to grow your money and keep it accessible. It can look like this chart.

Account Type	Interest	Amount	Maturity
Savings account	1.00%	$3,000	None
30-day CD	1.25%	$3,000	May 1
3-month CD	1.50%	$2,500	July 1
6-month CD	2.00%	$2,500	October 1
9-month CD	2.50%	$2,500	January 1
12-month CD	3.00%	$2,500	April 1
15-month CD	3.50%	$2,000	July 1
18-month CD	4.00%	$2,000	October 1
Total		$20,000	

The CDs roll over into a new term if the money is not withdrawn. For instance, if your six-month CD matures and you do nothing, it'll renew into another six-month CD with the current interest rate offered.

It's good to know this: financial institutions compete for deposits, so shop around for the best CD interest rates. Alternatively, you can choose to have certificates (CDs) with your primary bank or credit union for simplicity.

CD laddering is a good option for the Opportunity Fund and Cash Reserve you read about in the Manage Money pillar. Since balances tend to be higher in those accounts, you can earn a bit more using certificates.

You might wonder if it's better to put large amounts of money in the stock market for better returns. While I do believe you should earn more, it's also important to feel at ease knowing that some money is accessible and at lower risks. That is peace of mind.

Also, be mindful of social media money gurus focusing on maximization and encouraging you to save every penny in the stock market. I don't subscribe to that financial philosophy. The strategy you're learning is to save money for short-term use and invest money for long-term wealth. You may want to highlight this: don't get tempted to maximize your returns using the stock market. Your savings are for short-term use and need to remain accessible and not at the risk of daily market volatility.

TAKE ACTION

1. Review your savings accounts and decide if a better alternative exists. Use the worksheet found in the Appendix.

 Build Your Investments Recap

In this chapter, you learned why investing is something you must start today and how it's not as complicated as it may seem. The reality is that you're probably investing already by saving money into an interest-bearing account. The lessons you learned were found in these steps:

- **Step 1:** Getting started with investing
- **Step 2:** Compounding your returns
- **Step 3:** Earning more on savings

Remember, time is your friend when it comes to growing your money. Through compound interest and growth, your money starts to work for you.

Congrats! You've learned where to store your money for short-term use and better returns. In the next chapter, you'll learn to think long term and plan your retirement.

8

Contribute to Your Retirement

You're never too young to start planning and investing for retirement. In fact, starting sooner will require less money and help you take advantage of the power of time.

Your retirement plan starts with a vision of the lifestyle you want to live during your golden years, then determining how much money is needed for those years. Whether you think of retirement as a time for passion projects or more time with family and friends, you'll need to invest and make money grow to afford your retirement lifestyle.

For instance, if your retirement goal is $1,000,000 and you can contribute $1,000 per month, it would take you over 83 years to reach your goal. In contrast, if you invested $1,000 each month, it would take only 28 years (using a 7% return). The message is clear: it will take significantly fewer years to reach one million dollars through investing than saving.

It's even better to use tax-advantaged accounts for your retirement nest egg. In this chapter, you will learn all the retirement planning steps:

- **Step 1:** Planning your retirement lifestyle
- **Step 2:** Calculating your retirement needs
- **Step 3:** Participating in a 401(k) plan
- **Step 4:** Getting the employer match
- **Step 5:** Using target date funds
- **Step 6:** Using a Roth IRA for tax-free growth
- **Step 7:** Opening a Roth IRA account

STEP 1: PLANNING YOUR RETIREMENT LIFESTYLE

What is retirement anyway? According to www.merriam-webster.com, it's traditionally defined as "withdrawal from one's position or occupation or from active working life." In reality, many people define retirement as the point in life where they get to use their time however they want. Some people picture themselves sitting on a beach, playing with their grandkids, or working on hobbies, and some might find themselves traveling. How I envision my retirement may be quite different from yours.

How are you picturing your retirement? Give yourself some time to answer the question. You don't need all the details, but an overall big picture will help you plan better.

Okay, humor me a bit. Close your eyes and envision your retirement. What images come to mind? Where are you? Who are you with? What are you doing? All these things play a role in retiring the smile lifestyle way.

Now, I do want to acknowledge that it might be difficult to think about a future that is decades away. It's also challenging when you're still working to achieve near-term financial goals. But this is a crucial step. You need a destination to aim towards. Of course, as you live life, the ideal retirement lifestyle might change. It certainly has for me.

Write down your retirement goals. You can use the worksheet in the Appendix to help you identify them.

HOW TIME AFFECTS YOUR RETIREMENT PLANNING

The earlier you start investing for retirement, the more time your money has to grow. As an example, let's take three friends, Oscar, Hugo, and Leo. They are all the same age, graduated college the same year, and got jobs that paid $60,000 per year.

As part of retirement planning, they invested using a Roth IRA but started at different times.

- Oscar started contributing $6,000 (10% of his gross salary) into a Roth IRA annually at age 22. He contributed $240,000 by the time he retired at age 60.

- Hugo waited until he was 30 to start contributing. He contributed $6,000 per year until he retired at age 60, totaling $180,000.

- Leo waited until he was 40 to start contributing. He contributed $6,000 per year until he retired at age 60, for a total investment of $120,000.

Look at the graph to see the sizeable difference in portfolio growth.

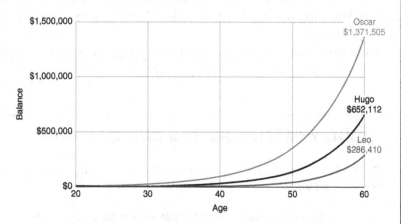

This example is for illustrative purposes only, assuming a moderate 7% return rate on your stock market investments. The historic annualized average return of the S&P 500 is around 10.5% since its inception in 1957.
Source: Adapted from https://www.spglobal.com/.

After 40 years, Oscar's total contribution has grown to $1,371,505. Hugo, who waited 10 years to start, has grown his portfolio to $652,112. And Leo, who chose to wait even longer, saw his 20 years of contributions grow to $286,410.

(*Continued*)

(*Continued*)

As you can see, the longer you wait to start investing the less time your money has to grow, and the smaller your retirement portfolio will be. With the Roth IRA, there are tax advantages. You'll learn more in step 6, "Using a Roth IRA for Tax-Free Growth."

STEP 2: CALCULATING YOUR RETIREMENT NEEDS

How much will you need for retirement? It really depends on the lifestyle you envision and how much that will cost. It's important to note that prices will increase, and you can factor that into your retirement budget. It's also good to understand that larger expenses such as a mortgage, student loans, and childcare may no longer exist, freeing a good portion of your income.

An easy way of calculating your retirement goal is to use your current lifestyle expenses as a benchmark. For example, if your current lifestyle is about $50,000 per year and you don't expect that to change, you can project your annual lifestyle expense in retirement to be $50,000 as well.

Now, take your projected annual lifestyle expense and multiply that by 25 to arrive at your retirement goal.

ESTIMATE YOUR RETIREMENT GOAL USING THE RULE OF 25

The rule of 25 is a helpful way to determine how much money you'll need at retirement. Use the following equation:

Retirement Goal = Annual Lifestyle Expense × 25

With a $50,000 projected lifestyle expense, you'll need about $1,250,000 saved.

Projected Annual Lifestyle Expense	Multiply by 25	Retirement Goal
$50,000	x 25	$1,250,000

Now, it's your turn: Calculate your projected lifestyle expense in retirement to determine your retirement goal.

Projected Annual Lifestyle Expense	Multiply by 25	Retirement Goal
$	x 25	$

If your retirement goal seems inflated because of your current lifestyle, reimagine the lifestyle of your dreams. You have control over your future lifestyle expenses.

How Much Do You Need to Reach Your Retirement Goal?

Let's continue with the example given. With the $1,250,000 retirement goal, it may take you 30 or 40 years to reach it.

If you are 20 years old, starting with $1,000 and contributing $500 per month, it will take you 40 years to reach $1.25 million. This assumes an expected annual rate of return of 7%. This chart shows how the money will grow over time.

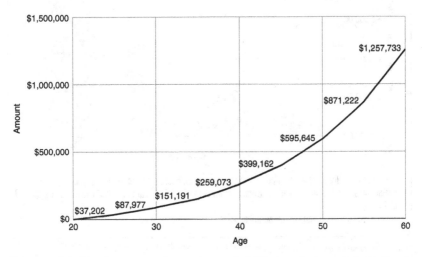

This example is for illustrative purposes only, assuming a moderate 7% return rate on your stock market investments. The historic annualized average return of the S&P 500 is around 10.5% since its inception in 1957. *Source:* Adapted from https://www.spglobal.com/.

If you're older, it's still possible to achieve the retirement goal. You'll need a larger starting amount, higher monthly contributions, and a higher earning rate than 7%.

Here's another example: Depending on the age you start and assuming an annual rate of return of 7%, you'll need to invest the following amount monthly to reach the retirement goal of $1.25 million by age 65.

- Starting at age 25: $515.13
- Starting at age 35: $1,096.03
- Starting at age 45: $2,533.06
- Starting at age 50: $4,136.12

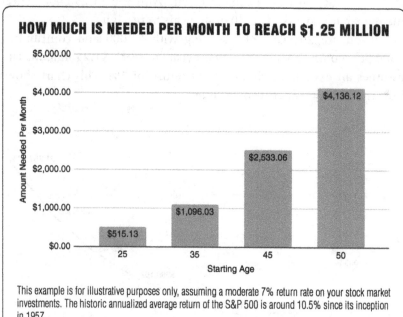

HOW MUCH IS NEEDED PER MONTH TO REACH $1.25 MILLION

This example is for illustrative purposes only, assuming a moderate 7% return rate on your stock market investments. The historic annualized average return of the S&P 500 is around 10.5% since its inception in 1957.
Source: Adapted from https://www.spglobal.com/.

Here's an important note. What I've shared are examples and may not apply to your specific situation. As I've repeated many times in this book, the answer to your particular circumstances will always start with "it depends," because how much you need and how much to contribute requires understanding the unique variables that play a role in your life.

Want to calculate how much you'll need to invest each month to reach your retirement goal? You're in luck. There are many online retirement calculators available. Go to investor.gov or visit thesmilemoney.com/book for updated resources.

If you went ahead and calculated your retirement goal and saw how much you need to invest each month and your anxiety shot up, allow yourself to feel that emotion. Sit with it for a moment. Give yourself some grace and space. Take a deep inhale through your nose and slowly exhale.

It may seem insurmountable, but it's also possible you've already made headway. For instance, your Social Security retirement benefits and contributions to an employer-sponsored plan, like a 401(k), can mean you're on track for retirement.

THINK ABOUT YOUR SOCIAL SECURITY RETIRE-MENT BENEFITS

I discussed Social Security Benefits Statements in the Earn Money pillar. But it's worth reminding you about them.

Social Security retirement benefits are an important part of your retirement income plan. You can view your earnings records and work credits through the Social Security Statement, which is available to everyone 25 years and over.

The SSA statement also shows your projected benefits payment upon retirement or disability. To create an account and view your statement, visit the Social Security Administration website at ssa.gov.

Now that you have an idea of how much you might need for retirement, we'll go over how to invest to reach that goal.

STEP 3: PARTICIPATING IN A 401(K) PLAN

There's a simple way to invest using tax-advantaged retirement accounts.

I was sitting at my desk at work when the credit union's financial advisor approached me and casually said, "Are you enrolled in the

401(k)?" I nodded a yes. Months ago, I had filled out all the forms during new-hire orientation.

"Don't do less than 10%," she said with her Australian accent, "You won't even realize the difference in your pay. You'll thank me later."

And I am thankful she said what she said. I love sharing this story over and over because it was life-changing advice that I wasn't expecting. At 22 years old, I wasn't thinking about what my life would be like at 70.

I'm taking her lead to emphasize participating in your 401(k) plan and doing what you can to contribute at least 10% of your pre-tax income.

Just like when she looked directly into my eyes and said, "Don't question it. Just do it," I also want you to "just do it." I say this knowing circumstances are different for each of us. But I do want you to grasp the importance of why you should.

Maybe you're already contributing to a 401(k) plan but are still unsure of how they work. Perhaps, you've heard of them and are wary of using them. I'm here to shed some light.

What Is a 401(k) Plan?

This is a retirement savings plan offered by employers. 401(k)s are defined contribution plans, which means that the amount of money you receive in retirement will depend on how much you contribute and how well your investments perform.

CPA and tax planning expert Yaroslav Tashak says, "With a 401(k), you can contribute pre-tax money from your paycheck, which can lower your taxable income. Your contributions and any earnings will not be taxed until you withdraw them in retirement."

You decide how much to contribute to your 401(k), up to the annual contribution limit set by the IRS. You can also choose how to invest your money from a variety of options that may include stocks, bonds, and mutual funds offered in the plan. Also, after changing jobs, you can take your money and roll it over into another retirement plan.

Contribution Limits	Visit irs.gov for the latest annual contribution limits.
Investment Choices	Choose from various stocks and funds offered in the 401(k) plan.

Some additional benefits of participating include:

- **Tax-advantaged.** Contributing to a pre-tax 401(k) might lower your tax liability by affecting your gross income. You pay taxes when you withdraw the money at retirement, with the earliest at 59.5 years old.

- **Protected.** If your finances sour, your retirement plan is protected from creditors or judgments. The Employee Retirement Income Security Act of 1974 (ERISA) protects your qualified retirement plan from claims.

- **Extra money.** Many employers match 401(k) contributions either on a dollar-for-dollar basis or as a percentage of your contributions. You want to contribute at least to the match so you don't leave money on the table.

WHAT ABOUT OTHER RETIREMENT PLANS?

403(b) and 457(b) plans

403(b) and 457(b) plans are similar to 401(k) plans in that they are all tax-deferred retirement savings plans offered by employers. However, there are some key differences among the three plans:

- 401(k) plans are offered by for-profit companies, while 403(b) plans are offered by nonprofit organizations such as schools and hospitals.
- 457(b) plans are offered by government entities.

The contribution limits, investment options, and withdrawal rules for 403(b) and 457(b) plans are different from those for 401(k) plans.

For up-to-date and more information on 403(b) and 457(b) plans, visit the IRS website at irs.gov.

Thrift Savings Plan (TSP)

TSP is a retirement savings plan available to federal employees, including military members. The TSP offers a variety of investment options, including stocks, bonds, and funds.

Military members can contribute up to 5% of their pay to the TSP, and the government matches 50% of their contributions up to 6% of their pay. The TSP is a

(Continued)

(*Continued*)

great way for military members to save for retirement and offers several advantages over other retirement savings plans.

Here are some of the advantages of the TSP:

- It is a tax-deferred account, which means that you do not pay taxes on your contributions or earnings until you withdraw them.
- It is a low-cost investment option, with fees that are significantly lower than those of many other retirement savings plans.
- It is a portable account, which means that you can take it with you if you change jobs or retire.
- It is a secure account, with the government backing your investments.

If you are a military member, the TSP is a great way to save for retirement. It is a simple, low-cost, and secure way to save for your future.

For more, visit the Thrift Savings Plan website at tsp.gov.

STEP 4: GETTING THE EMPLOYER MATCH

Many employers offer a 401(k) match, which is a contribution they make to your 401(k) account based on your contribution. The amount of the match varies by employer.

For example, an employer may match 50 cents for every dollar you contribute, up to a certain percentage of your salary (perhaps 3% to 6%). In this case, if you contributed $5,000 in a calendar year, your company would match it with $2,500. This matching contribution is essentially part of your earnings, so you should take it. Not contributing to your 401(k) to at least the employer match leaves money on the table. It's a decision that affects your financial well-being.

HOW AN EMPLOYER MATCH AFFECTS YOUR 401(K) BALANCE

To further illustrate, let's say your employer matches 50% of contributions. You contribute 6% of your gross income and the employer matches with 3%. In total, your retirement contribution is 9%. With an 8–10% average annual return, your 401(k) balance will grow. Look at the example in the chart to see how it all works.

Age	Salary	Your 6% Contribution	3% Employer Match	Total Con- tributions	Year-end 401(k) Balance
21	$30,000	$1,800	$900	$2,700	$2,889.00
22	$30,900	$1,854	$927	$2,781	$6,123.60
23	$31,827	$1,910	$955	$2,864	$9,707.07
24	$32,781	$1,967	$983	$2,950	$13,670.03
25	$33,765	$2,026	$1,013	$3,039	$18,045.62
26	$34,778	$2,087	$1,043	$3,130	$22,869.71
27	$35,822	$2,149	$1,075	$3,224	$28,181.14
28	$36,896	$2,214	$1,107	$3,321	$34,021.95
29	$38,003	$2,280	$1,140	$3,420	$40,437.60

This example is for illustrative purposes only, assuming a moderate 7% return rate on your stock market investments. The historic annualized average return of the S&P 500 is around 10.5% since its inception in 1957.
Source: Adapted from https://www.spglobal.com/.

I want to reemphasize how vital it is to contribute at least the amount of the full match. Otherwise you're saying "no thanks" to money that belongs to you. And if you can, try upping your contribution to 10%. I also challenge you to aim a bit higher: think 15–20%. Optimistically, consider contributing as much as you can up to the limits set by the IRS. You'll thank me later.

STEP 5: USING TARGET DATE FUNDS

Take the guesswork out of your retirement plan investments. Most 401(k) plans offer target-date funds. Target date funds are a type of mutual fund that invests in a mix of stocks, bonds, and other assets.

A target-date fund is a strategy that rebalances your investments over time. When you're younger, with a longer retirement timeline, your money is invested heavily in stocks. As you near retirement age, it switches over to bonds. The fund's investment mix becomes more conservative as the target date approaches, which reduces exposure to market volatility right around the age you'll need the money to pay for living expenses.

The target-date fund is named after the expected decade of retirement. You might see the funds named 2040, 2050, or 2060, and so on.

When choosing a target date fund, it's important to consider your retirement goals and your risk tolerance. You should also choose a fund that has a target date that is close to your expected retirement date.

Let's say you're a 30-year-old in 2024, which gives you about 37 more years before reaching the traditional retirement age. At age 67, it will be 2061, so choosing a 2060 target-date fund is ideal.

Target date funds are a popular choice for retirement savings because they are easy to use and offer a diversified investment strategy. And if you're not comfortable managing your own investments, it's a good option to choose. This was the option I chose.

WHAT IS RETIREMENT ASSET ALLOCATION?

Asset allocation is an investment strategy recommending how much money to put in stocks, bonds, and cash when investing for retirement. The goal is to proportion these three types of asset classes. As you age, your risk is adjusted to a conservative mix in favor of fixed-income investments such as bonds.

The following is a simple asset allocation recommended by T. Rowe Price based on age. It does not take into account your time horizon or personal risk tolerance, but it's still a good guide to understand how it all works.

- **20s:** 90% to 100% equity, zero to 10% bonds
- **30s:** 90% to 100% equity, zero to 10% bonds
- **40s:** 80% to 100% equity, zero to 20% bonds
- **50s:** 65% to 85% equity, 15% to 35% bonds
- **60s:** 45% to 65% equity, 30% to 50% bonds, zero to 10% cash/cash-equivalents
- **70+:** 30% to 50% equity, 40% to 60% bonds, zero to 20% cash/cash-equivalents

As you can see from this example, the investments are reallocated as you get closer to traditional retirement age. It's important to understand that your personal situation matters, and speaking with an investment advisor or financial planner can be helpful.

Source: Adapted from *T. Rowe Price,* https://www.troweprice.com/personal-investing/resources/planning/asset-allocation-planning.html.

STEP 6: USING A ROTH IRA FOR TAX-FREE GROWTH

Use another tax-advantage retirement account to save even more. If you have the means, having both a 401(k) and a Roth IRA can offer unique advantages in building a diversified and tax-efficient retirement portfolio.

Let's start with some basics.

IRA stands for Individual Retirement Arrangement, and it is a government-sponsored program that offers multiple investment options for your retirement savings.

There are two main types of IRAs: traditional and Roth. Traditional IRAs allow you to deduct your contributions from your taxes in the year you make them. In contrast, Roth IRAs do not offer a tax deduction upfront but allow your money to grow tax-free. There are contribution limits each year for both traditional and Roth IRAs. And if you're 50 years and older, there is a catch-up provision allowing you to contribute a bit more.

Let me explain in greater detail.

The **traditional IRA** contributions are made pre-tax, often lowering your taxable income like a pre-tax 401(k) plan. Your investments in a traditional IRA grow tax-deferred. You will only have to pay income taxes when you withdraw from the traditional IRA after you retire. A traditional IRA can be opened by an individual regardless of employment. It's also the best option for self-employed and independent contractors.

If you choose a **Roth IRA**, you can invest after-tax money up to a certain amount each year. However, your contributions will not be tax-deductible. Instead, the earnings and future withdrawals from the Roth IRA are tax-free after you reach 59.5 years old. Again, your money in a Roth IRA grows tax-free.

Here is a table summarizing the features and benefits of traditional and Roth IRAs.

Feature	Traditional IRA	Roth IRA
Tax deduction	Yes	No
Tax-free growth	No	Yes
Required minimum distribution	Yes	No
Withdrawals	Taxable	Tax-free

The next table explains a bit more about the pros and cons.

Roth IRA	Traditional IRA
Pros	**Pros**
▪ Because of after-tax contributions, your investments grow tax-free.	▪ Your contributions can reduce the taxable income in the year they were made if they are deductible.
▪ Withdraw your money from a Roth IRA without taxes and penalties at any time without stating a reason. Only available if you made your first contribution at least 5 years ago or if your age is 59½.	▪ Potential earnings will grow tax-deferred.
▪ It's not mandatory to withdraw a minimum amount from a Roth IRA, no matter your age.	▪ You can use your money without any penalty after age 59½.
▪ You can keep your money in your Roth IRA for as long as you wish to grow without being taxed.	▪ You're not taxed until you reach retirement and withdraw the money.
	▪ There is no income limit.
Cons	**Cons**
▪ You cannot use a Roth IRA if your income exceeds the IRS limit.	▪ If you take money out of a traditional IRA before retirement, you will have to pay income taxes on gains and taxable contributions.
▪ No immediate tax benefits when making contributions.	▪ Early withdrawal will cost you a 10% penalty.
▪ If you want to withdraw your earnings (not contributions) early, you might have to pay a 10% penalty or income taxes unless there's an exception.	▪ After age 72, you will need to withdraw a minimum amount of money, called an RMD (required minimum distribution).

As you can see, there are pros and cons to both types of IRAs. The best type of IRA for you will depend on your individual circumstances. If you are unsure which type of IRA is right for you, consult a tax professional or financial planner with tax planning experience. The best source for updated information is found on the IRS website by visiting irs.gov.

But Why Invest Using a Roth IRA?

Because you've already paid taxes on the money in your Roth IRA, you don't have to pay taxes again when you take it out in retirement. Another benefit is that there are no required minimum distributions, like forced withdrawals, while you're alive. This allows your account to keep growing for as long as you want.

Now, here's what I recommend: Have both the tax-deferred 401(k) and tax-free Roth IRA for your retirement. It diversifies your income sources, and it gives you more flexibility in managing taxes during retirement. It also provides a hedge against potential changes in tax laws, giving you the ability to choose which account to withdraw from based on your financial situation each year.

With the benefits of Roth IRAs, you'd think everyone would take advantage of them. Well, high-income earners want to but aren't eligible.

So What Makes You Ineligible for Roth IRAS?

Your eligibility to contribute to a Roth IRA hinges on your income, known as the Modified Adjusted Gross Income (MAGI). The IRS sets different income ranges each year, and your eligibility depends on where your MAGI falls within those ranges and your tax filing status.

For example, in 2024, the upper-income limits are:

- $161,000 for individuals filing taxes as single
- $240,000 for married couples filing jointly

If your MAGI exceeds the upper limit of the range, you are not eligible to contribute to a Roth IRA for that tax year. If your MAGI fall below the upper limit, you're eligible to contribute the maximum or partial amount based on your income level for that tax year.

Knowing these income limits is crucial because they can change annually. If your income surpasses the Roth IRA limits, you have some alternatives:

- **Consider contributing to a traditional IRA**. You can still make nondeductible contributions to a traditional IRA regardless of your income.
- **Then use a Backdoor Roth IRA:** This strategy involves making a nondeductible contribution to a traditional IRA and then converting it to a Roth IRA. It's a good option if you don't have any other traditional IRA assets, as it can help you avoid the pro-rata rule. That rule determines the taxable portion of the conversion based on the mix of pre-tax and after-tax money in your IRAs. It can get confusing, so get help from a tax professional who understands Backdoor Roth IRAs.

STEP 7: OPENING A ROTH IRA ACCOUNT

Let's start your Roth IRA investments. Now that you've gotten a better understanding of Roth IRAs, you'll want to choose where to open an account.

When you open an IRA at a bank or credit union, it typically comes with an interest rate similar to a savings account. On the other hand, opting for a brokerage account provides more investment choices, which could yield higher returns. It's worth noting that some banks and credit unions work with investment firms to offer IRAs through their brokerage services. You can find the best brokerages by visiting the resource page at thesmilemoney.com/book.

After opening your Roth IRA, you'll need to deposit money into the account. The funds will need to settle (banking jargon that means "made available") before you can invest the money. You'll learn more about the different investments you can choose in Chapter 9, "Invest for Independence," because it's a similar process.

Now, make sure to double-check that the money in the IRA was invested.

Here's a word of caution from Kevin Matthews II of buildingbread.com: "Don't make the mistake of depositing your money into the Roth account and forgetting to invest it."

I've seen this happen before. People are excited about the benefits of Roths and will open an account, deposit the money, and forget to invest it. So the funds have been sitting there uninvested.

"Think of your IRA as a car, but you'll need gas to drive it," Kevin says. "The investments you choose—stocks or index funds—is the gas." Your money sitting in an IRA won't go anywhere if you haven't invested it.

You'll need to decide where to invest using stocks, index funds, ETFs, or a combination of them. I'll cover this in the next chapter.

To recap this step: 1) find a brokerage firm; 2) open a Roth IRA account; 3) deposit money and wait for it to settle; 4) choose your investments; 5) double-check to ensure money was invested.

And congrats! You've just finished a hefty chapter on investing for retirement. Be proud of yourself. You're on track to retiring with a smile.

TAKE ACTION

Use the worksheet in the Appendix to help you complete the exercises:

1. Calculate your retirement goal: how much do you need?
2. Participate in the 401(k) plan and set your contribution percentage.
3. Contribute the minimum to get the full employer match.
4. Determine if a Roth IRA can work for you.
5. Review your projected Social Security Benefits.

 Contribute to Your Retirement Recap

We will all retire one day, whether by choice, age, or illness. Starting early allows you to choose when to retire rather than waiting until the full retirement age set by the government. Retirement planning is crucial for your well-being. It'll give you peace of mind about the future.

(*Continued*)

(Continued)

In this chapter, you were introduced to the rule of 25 to calculate your retirement number and learned the importance of taking advantage of employer benefits and tax-advantaged retirement savings. You learned the key retirement planning steps:

- **Step 1:** Planning your retirement lifestyle
- **Step 2:** Calculating your retirement needs
- **Step 3:** Participating in a 401(k) plan
- **Step 4:** Getting the employer match
- **Step 5:** Using target date funds
- **Step 6:** Using a Roth IRA for tax-free growth
- **Step 7:** Opening a Roth IRA account

You now have the knowledge and resources to plan for retirement successfully.

Woohoo! You finished the lessons to help you reach retirement. In the next chapter, I'm going to help you invest for financial independence and teach you the steps to a work-optional lifestyle.

CHAPTER **9**

Invest
for Independence

Start investing to free yourself.

You don't have to wait for traditional retirement to live your dream life. I want you to regain your time freedom much sooner. You can do this by intentionally investing with the goal of independence.

I started investing in the stock market (outside of a retirement plan) in my late 20s. Unfortunately, I didn't have a strategy. It led to losses and caused more headaches and made me believe investing wasn't for me. Fortunately, I learned investing *was* for me. The key to investing success was intentionality. What are the intentions for the wealth I wanted to create? My intention was to regain my time and live life on my terms. Investing for my independence was the answer.

How are you investing? What are your intentions? It's vital to think long-term when it comes to investing for financial independence. And I'll show you how to invest intentionally in six steps:

- **Step 1:** Starting with investing fundamentals
- **Step 2:** Calculating your financial independence number

- **Step 3:** Determining how much to invest
- **Step 4:** Opening a brokerage account
- **Step 5:** Choosing an investment activity
- **Step 6:** Automating your investing

As you progress through the steps, I want you to consider your situation, goals, and values to customize the strategy to meet your needs. And once again, the type of investments you'll need to make will depend on your personal time horizon and risk tolerance. What may work for some may not work for you. But I do want you to know I created these steps with flexibility and customizability to meet your personal needs.

STEP 1: STARTING WITH INVESTING FUNDAMENTALS

Knowing more about investing increases the odds you'll continue to invest. So we're going to start with the fundamentals.

First, there is a difference between investing, trading, speculating, and gambling in the stock market. It's essential to know this.

Investing in the stock market involves buying and holding stocks for an extended period, often for long-term growth and building wealth. In contrast, **day trading** involves navigating volatile stock markets to seize opportunities in the short term. **Speculating** focuses on hype rather than company performance. And **gambling** relies on impulsive decisions without considering any fundamentals. Each approach carries its own risks and potential rewards.

Second, there are different investing approaches, but we'll stick with the method that works for most successful investors. This means showing you how to invest in low-cost index funds and ETFs, as opposed to actively trading stocks. In the following steps, you'll learn more about how to reach financial independence using a passive investing method.

WHAT TYPE OF INVESTMENTS ARE THERE?

Here's a breakdown of the different investment options available in the stock market.

Stocks

When you invest in stocks, you become a partial owner of a publicly traded company. It's like owning a small piece of the business. Companies issue shares of stock to raise money for operations or growth. As a shareholder, you have the potential to benefit from the company's success through dividends and stock price appreciation.

Bonds

On the other hand, bonds are more like loans. When you buy a bond, you lend money to a government, municipality, or corporation. They promise to repay the loan amount and interest at a fixed rate over a specified period.

Mutual Funds

Mutual funds offer a diversified approach to investing. They pool money from many investors to buy a mix of stocks, bonds, and other assets. You buy shares in the mutual fund, representing your ownership in the fund's portfolio. Although they may have higher fees due to active management, mutual funds provide professional oversight and a broad range of investment opportunities.

Index Funds

By investing in an index fund, you can gain exposure to a whole group of stocks without managing individual stocks yourself. These funds aim to match the performance of a specific market index, like the famous S&P 500. If you prefer a more passive investment strategy, index funds are worth considering.

Exchange-Traded Funds

ETFs are an interesting option. They're similar to mutual funds but trade on the stock exchange throughout the day like regular stocks. Some ETFs also track market indexes (Index ETFs), making ETFs a cost-effective way to invest in a diversified basket of stocks.

(Continued)

(*Continued*)
Real Estate Investment Trusts (REITs)

You can participate in the real estate market without the hassle of owning physical properties. These companies own or finance income-generating real estate properties, benefiting you from the potential rental income and property appreciation.

Commodities

This is another way to diversify your investment portfolio. Commodities include physical goods like gold, silver, oil, and agricultural products. You can gain exposure to commodities through ETFs and mutual funds, allowing you to tap into potential price movements in these assets.

STEP 2: CALCULATING YOUR FINANCIAL INDEPENDENCE NUMBER

Let's start by having you envision a financially independent life where work is optional. Refer back to the envisioning exercise in Chapter 8, "Contribute to Your Retirement." I want you to know that investing for independence is simply about accelerating your path to retirement. Instead of investing for 30 years, you invest more of your income, allowing you to "retire" much sooner.

So, how much do you need? It depends on the lifestyle you want to live. But there are three things you can do:

1. Calculate the cost of your current lifestyle and use the rule of 25 to arrive at your financial independence (FI) number.

2. Take your projected living expenses from your retirement calculation to get your FI number.

3. Use the standard $1,000,000 target set by many financial independence seekers.

To illustrate this step, use "your current lifestyle expenses" to calculate your FI number in this exercise.

HOW TO CALCULATE YOUR FI NUMBER

Here's the first part: To get your FI number, you'll need your monthly expenses multiplied by 12 (months). As an example, let's use $3,333 as a monthly expense.

Monthly Expenses × 12 = Total Yearly Expenses

Monthly Expenses	Multiply	12 Months	Equals	Total Yearly Expenses
$3,333	x	12	=	$40,000

Now it's your turn: Calculate your total yearly expenses.

Monthly Expenses	Multiply	12 Months	Equals	Total Yearly Expenses
$	x	12	=	$

Here's the second part: Use the rule of 25. Look at your total yearly expenses and multiply that by 25.

Financial Independence Number = Yearly Expenses × 25

For example, if your total yearly expenses equal $40,000, you'll need $1,000,000 ($40,000×25) saved.

Give it a try: How much do you need saved? What is your FI number?

Yearly Expenses	Multiply	25	Equals	FI Number
$40,000	x	25	=	$1,000,000
$	x	25	=	$

Remember, the lower your monthly expenses, the lower your FI number can be.

After calculating your financial independence number, you might feel a sense of relief knowing you're on track. Or you might be feeling stressed about the impossibility of reaching that goal. Take a moment to collect your thoughts. Take a deep intentional breath. It may seem impossible, but not improbable. With the right strategy, you might achieve the unthinkable—your financial independence.

Can you really live off your investments?

Again, the answer will begin with "it depends." Changes in your lifestyle or economic market conditions can impact your investments. However, following the 4% rule can help you live off your investments in perpetuity.

The **4% rule** is the most common rule followed by the financial independence community. It is based on the Trinity Study,[1] which found that the rule applies regardless of market fluctuations. The rule states that you can safely withdraw 4% of the value of your investments during your first year of financial independence. You can then withdraw the same dollar amount, adjusted for inflation, in the following years. If you withdraw no more than 4% of your investments each year, your assets should last for the rest of your life. The 4% rule is often referred to as the safe withdrawal rate, or SWR.

HOW MUCH CAN YOU WITHDRAW?

For instance, your $1,000,000 investment allows you to withdraw $40,000 annually and indefinitely when using the 4% rule or safe withdrawal rate (SWR).

Investment Portfolio	Multiply	4%	Equals	Safe Withdrawal Amount
$1,000,000	x	0.04 or 4%	=	$40,000

Now, it's your turn: Calculate how much you can safely withdraw. Use the FI number you calculated earlier.

Investment Portfolio	Multiply	4%	Equals	Safe Withdrawal Amount
$	x	0.04 or 4%	=	$

Now, once your **Investment Portfolio** reaches your **FI Number**, you're able to live off your investments and can **safely withdraw** money to pay for **Yearly Expenses**.

---

[1] Trinity Study, https://en.wikipedia.org/wiki/Trinity_study.

Did you notice something? The 4% rule and the rule of 25 are related. Both calculations can help you arrive at the same conclusion. It just takes different approaches.

Keep this in mind: If your current investment portfolio is far from your FI number, you'll need to determine how much more to invest to reach financial independence sooner.

STEP 3: DETERMINING HOW MUCH TO INVEST

How much you need to invest depends on how fast you want to reach your goals.

The chart shown here illustrates how investing 10% of your income will grow in 30 years, giving you an idea of the income contribution needed for investments. This contribution table applies to retirement planning as well.

Income	Yearly Contribution (10% of income)	Value in 30 Years*
$35,000	$3,500	$357,256
$50,000	$5,000	$510,365
$60,000	$6,000	$612,438
$70,000	$7,000	$714,511
$80,000	$8,000	$816,584
$90,000	$9,000	$918,657
$100,000	$10,000	$1,020,730
$120,000	$12,000	$1,224,876
$150,000	$15,000	$1,531,096
$200,000	$20,000	$2,041,461

*This example is for illustrative purposes only, assuming a moderate 7% return rate on your stock market investments. The historic annualized average return of the S&P 500 is around 10.5% since its inception in 1957.
Source: Adapted from https://www.spglobal.com/

To better illustrate, here's an example. Let's say your FI number is $1,000,000. Starting at age 25, you'll need to invest $363 per month for the next 40 years to grow your investments to $1 million by age 65. This calculation assumes an annual rate of return of 7% and a starting portfolio of $4,661 ($363 × 12) invested in the first year.

If you decide to start later than 25 years old, you'll need to invest more than $363 per month. Your monthly investment amount will increase to the following:

- Starting at age 35: $820
- Starting at age 45: $1,924
- Starting at age 50: $3,115

The later you start, the more you'll need to invest each month to reach a million dollars. And as you've read in Chapter 7, "Build Your Investments," investing sooner is to your benefit.

So how can you reach financial independence sooner regardless of age? You must invest more. Now, going back to the example, if you're 25 years old and investing $363 per month, you could double that amount to $726. It would result in reaching the $1 million FI number at age 55, about 10 years earlier.

Now, let's take a look at the contribution table again. Look at the impact of increasing your yearly contribution from 10% to 15%.

Income	Yearly Contribution (10% of income)	Value in 30 Years*	Yearly Contribution (15% of income)	Value in 30 Years*
$35,000	$3,500	$357,256	$5,250	$535,883
$50,000	$5,000	$510,365	$7,500	$765,548
$60,000	$6,000	$612,438	$9,000	$918,657
$70,000	$7,000	$714,511	$10,500	$1,071,767
$80,000	$8,000	$816,584	$12,000	$1,224,876
$90,000	$9,000	$918,657	$13,500	$1,377,986
$100,000	$10,000	$1,020,730	$15,000	$1,531,096
$120,000	$12,000	$1,224,876	$18,000	$1,837,315
$150,000	$15,000	$1,531,096	$22,500	$2,296,643
$200,000	$20,000	$2,041,461	$30,000	$3,062,191

*This example is for illustrative purposes only, assuming a moderate 7% return rate on your stock market investments. The historic annualized average return of the S&P 500 is around 10.5% since its inception in 1957.
Source: Adapted from https://www.spglobal.com/

I don't want you stressing about all these numbers, because these are guidelines. Fortunately, many online calculators help estimate how much you'll need to reach your FI number. Visit the resource page on thesmilemoney.com/book for links to them.

HOW LONG WILL IT TAKE TO REACH FINANCIAL INDEPENDENCE?

If you enjoy calculations, use the following equation to estimate the time it'll take to reach FI.

Years to FI = (FI Number − Existing Portfolio Amount) / Yearly Savings

- **Existing Portfolio Amount:** The total amount of money already saved that includes retirement accounts, investable accounts (brokerage, stocks, etc.), pensions, and other savings accounts
- **Yearly Savings:** The amount of money you invest monthly multiplied by 12 months

For example, let's say your FI number is $1,000,000, and you already have $250,000 in existing investment portfolios. You would need to save $750,000 more to reach your number. Assuming you can save $25,000 annually, it would take you 30 years.

Your calculation would look like this:

($1,000,000 − $250,000) / $25,000 = 30 Years to FI

FI Number	Minus	Existing Portfolio Amount	Divided	Yearly Savings	Equals	Years to FI
$1,000,000	−	$250,000	÷	$25,000	=	30

This calculation is helpful but it's a simple one. It does not take into account the compound growth of investments. If your investments have an average 7% rate of return per year, you will reach FI in 12 years, not 30. That is the power of investing.

Now, it's your turn: How many years will it take to reach your FI number? Use the calculation to estimate.

FI Number	Minus	Existing Portfolio Amount	Divided	Yearly Savings	Equals	Years to FI
$	−	$	÷	$	=	

(Continued)

(*Continued*)

To try an online calculator using a 7% rate of return, go to thesmilemoney.com/book.

Online Calculator Estimate (Years to FI)	$

Compare the two. You'll notice the power of compounding and how that can take years off the path to financial independence.

Keep this in mind: You can reduce the Years to FI by increasing your monthly investing amount or by earning a higher rate of return.

Now that you know how much to invest, it's time to choose where to invest.

STEP 4: OPENING A BROKERAGE ACCOUNT

Are you the DIY type? If you want to choose the funds and stocks that make up your portfolio, you're a self-directed investor. All you need is a brokerage account offering a more hands-on approach. This isn't as frightening as it may seem.

On the other hand, if you want your investments managed with guidance, then human advisors or robo-advisory services would serve you well. This option is best for the done-for-you investor who wants expert advice and is okay with paying wealth management fees.

When comparing brokerages, consider factors such as minimum account requirements, costs, fees, the availability of investor research tools, and, if needed, access to human advisors. Let's focus on two popular online options.

■ **Option 1: Self-Directed (DIY) Brokerage Account**

A self-directed online brokerage account allows you to take control of your investments. You can begin investing, picking, and choosing the stocks and funds on your own. If you enjoy managing your investments and want more control over your portfolio, a self-directed brokerage account might be the right fit.

■ **Option 2: Robo-Advisor Brokerage Account**

A robo-advisor brokerage account offers a different approach. During the onboarding process, they'll ask about your financial goals and create a personalized investment portfolio. If you prefer a more hands-off approach and want expert guidance with lower fees, a robo-advisor could be a better choice.

Which option sounds the most appealing?

I want you to understand that you can use either option to invest for independence. At this step, it's a matter of preference and goals. Both options offer unique benefits. As you gain more investing experience, you can always reassess your brokerage account to ensure it continues to meet your needs.

What brokerage company should you use? There are many to choose from, including well-known names like Charles Schwab, Fidelity, and Vanguard. You can also find an updated list of the best online brokerages by visiting thesmilemoney.com/book.

DETERMINING WHAT BROKERAGE SERVICE YOU NEED

There are three services available:

An **online brokerage** is a digital platform enabling you to buy, sell, and manage investments like stocks, bonds, index funds, and ETFs. It offers a user-friendly interface to access financial markets, execute trades, monitor performance, and gather market research and analysis. Online brokerages offer reduced commissions and lower fees than traditional broker services.

A **robo-advisor** is a brokerage service that offers guided advice through an investment philosophy and proprietary algorithms. Robo-advisors can assist you with targeted retirement goals, college savings plans, tax-loss harvesting, portfolio rebalancing, 401(k) investment reviews, and other retirement accounts. You'll be asked questions about your goals, risk tolerance, age, and desired retirement. Based on your answers, its algorithms recommend a portfolio of stocks, bonds, and other investments.

A **wealth management service** offers comprehensive financial planning and personalized investment management for high-net-worth individuals and families. It goes beyond just investment advice and includes a broader range of services like

(Continued)

(Continued)

tax planning, estate planning, retirement planning, and risk management. Wealth managers work closely with clients to understand their specific financial goals, risk tolerance, and overall financial situation, and they create customized investment strategies and financial plans for clients.

How do you select the right brokerage service?

Ask yourself the following questions:

- Do I prefer a hands-on approach or a more automated, hands-off approach?
- How comfortable am I with managing my investments independently?
- Am I confident in making buy and sell decisions on my own?
- Do I have the time and interest to research and monitor investments regularly?
- How important is personalized guidance and advice in managing my investments?
- Am I looking for a cost-effective solution to execute trades, or am I willing to pay higher fees for additional services?
- Do I have complex financial needs like tax planning, estate planning, or risk management?
- What is my risk tolerance? Am I comfortable with potential fluctuations in the value of my investments?
- Do I have a specific retirement goal or other financial milestones I want to achieve?

Based on your answers, determine which aligns with your needs.

- If you **prefer more control** over your investments and have the time and knowledge to manage them independently, an online brokerage is the best choice.
- If you **want automated investment management** and guided advice based on your goals and risk tolerance, a robo-advisor could be suitable.
- If you **have complex financial needs** and a significant number of assets, and you desire personalized financial planning, a wealth management service may be the right option.

The choice is yours.

STEP 5: CHOOSING AN INVESTMENT ACTIVITY

After successfully opening your brokerage account, the next step is to determine your investment strategy. Although I encourage passive investing, I want you to know both approaches.

- **Approach 1: Active Investing**

  Active investing means choosing and managing investments to beat the market or a benchmark. Active investors research and analyze individual stocks, bonds, or other assets to make decisions based on their predictions. It's more hands-on, involving frequent buying and selling of shares based on predictions and pursuing higher returns.

- **Approach 2: Passive Investing**

  Passive investing aims to match a market index's performance, not to try and outperform it. Passive investors use index funds or exchange-traded funds (ETFs) that track the performance of a specific index, such as the S&P 500. Instead of constantly buying and selling, you hold on to investments to capture the overall market's growth over time. It generally has lower fees and involves less trading.

The Case for Passively Investing Using Index Funds

Did you know the historic annualized average return of the S&P 500 has been around 10.5% since its inception in 1957?[2] It's a reason the charts and graphs you've read in this pillar all use index funds as the driver for growth.

By investing in an index fund, you gain exposure to a broad range of stocks within that index. This inherent diversification reduces individual stock volatility and offers lower overall risks than investing in individual stocks.

Warren Buffett, often regarded as one of the most successful investors in the world, is an advocate of index funds. He famously said

[2]S&P Global, https://www.spglobal.com/.

low-cost index funds tracking the S&P 500 were the best investment for most Americans.[3] Buffett also said that if you believe in a company's long-term growth, choosing individual stocks can work out well. This is the basis of my Core and Explore investing strategy. Eighty percent of my investment portfolio (my core) is index funds and ETFs. The 20% (my explore) comprises stocks from companies with a track record of sustainable business practices, dividend payouts, and long-term growth potential. I don't day trade and won't speculate on risky assets as part of my investing for independence goals.

Just Keep It Simple

Avoid highly speculative investing, and don't chase the latest stock tip. Some people might have the talent to pick high-performing stocks, but they are outliers and probably spend their days analyzing the markets. Your goal should not be to beat the experts or time the market. Make your goal to simply be invested in the market. Make it easier on yourself and focus on the long-term growth of your investments.

Think Cheap, Stable, and Boring

Index funds are pretty dull. And that's a good thing. You're less affected by media hype associated with a stock's daily swings. Instead, you hold index funds well into your golden years, lowering your risks and ensuring your portfolio performs well, even in down markets.

My recommendation is this. Instead of trying to figure out what stocks to own, just own every single stock in that index. There's a benefit to doing so because it's more affordable and inherently diversified. It's also self-balancing because a publicly traded company is required to meet specific metrics to remain in the index. Underperformers are removed and replaced without you having to do anything.

Ultimately, the choice between active investing and passive investing with index funds is yours to make. Personally, I prefer taking the guesswork out of investing. Since learning how passive investors grow

[3]CNBC., https://www.cnbc.com/2021/05/03/investing-lessons-from-warren-buffett-at-berkshire-hathaway-meeting.html.

wealth, I've passively invested with index funds and ETFs for years now. The simplicity keeps me focused on having a more active lifestyle. It's like a set-it-and-forget-it approach. I choose my index funds and automate the monthly contributions.

HOW PASSIVELY INVESTING IN INDEX FUNDS WORKS

Here's an example of how investing $363 per month consistently into an index fund for 40 years will grow to $1,000,000 with a total investment of $174,240.

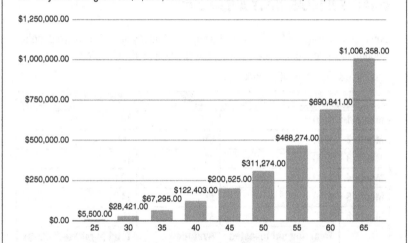

This example is for illustrative purposes only, assuming a moderate 7% return rate on your stock market investments. The historic annualized average return of the S&P 500 is around 10.5% since its inception in 1957.
Source: Adapted from https://www.spglobal.com/.

Investing later than 25 years old? As you've read about time and compounding, you'll simply need to invest more or extend your timeline.

STEP 6: AUTOMATING YOUR INVESTING

Don't time the market. Just be consistent through automation.

Remove the guesswork and make it easy for your money to grow. Schedule and automate your investments. It gives you consistency and frequency. You will benefit from the market ups and downs through dollar-cost averaging. Over time, the DCA strategy lowers your average cost per share compared to buying all the shares at once at a higher price.

You might be wondering, "Aren't markets volatile?" The stock market is unpredictable in the short term. But if you look long-term, you'll come to the realization that markets have a cycle of ups and downs and crashes. You shouldn't be afraid that crashes might happen because they *will* occur. Shift your mindset to realize that crashes are opportunities to buy shares of companies at a discount or a "sale price."

WHAT IS DOLLAR-COST AVERAGING?

Dollar-cost averaging (DCA) is a strategy of regularly investing a fixed dollar amount, regardless of the share price. DCA applies to individual stocks and funds. This table shows how DCA works.

Time	Amount	Share Price	Shares Purchased
Month 1	$100	$10	10
Month 2	$100	$10	10
Month 3	$100	$8	12
Month 4	$100	$5	20
Month 5	$100	$7	14
Month 6	$100	$10	10
	Total amount invested	Average cost per share	Total purchased shares
	$600	$8.33	76

In this example, DCA reduced the cost per share and enabled the purchase of 76 shares. If, in Month 1, you bought $600 worth of shares at $10, it would result in having only 60 shares.

Invest Small Amounts to Grow Your Portfolio

There is a misconception that you need a lot of money to start investing. Nothing could be further from the truth. You can start small, invest consistently, and build your portfolio over time. There are two methods you can use.

Method 1: Buying fractional shares

Fractional share investing is where investors buy a portion or a fraction of a share of a company's stock or fund rather than buying a full share. You can buy fractional shares through many online brokerages. It's an opportunity to own high-priced stocks by investing small amounts of money on a regular automatic basis.

It works this way: When you place an order for a fractional share, the brokerage will pool your investment with other investors' money and use it to purchase full shares of the stock. Then you'll be assigned a fraction of that full share, proportional to the amount of money you invested.

For example, let's say you want to invest in an index ETF that is currently trading at $1,000 per share, but you only have $250 to invest. With fractional share investing, you can invest $250 and own 0.25 shares of the index ETF. Many brokerages even allow you to buy shares starting at one dollar. In that case, your fractional share of one dollar would be equivalent to 0.001 shares of that index ETF.

Method 2: Enrolling in DRIP

Some companies offer Dividend Reinvestment Plans, allowing investors to automatically reinvest any dividends earned into purchasing additional shares of the same stock or fund.

For example, let's say you own 100 shares of a company's stock that pays a quarterly dividend of $0.50 per share. That would give you a total dividend payout of $50 every quarter. With DRIP, the dividend payout is automatically used to buy additional shares of the same stock.

DRIPs compound your investment over time without the need to reinvest the dividends yourself manually. This can help you accumulate more shares and increase your long-term returns. Many stocks and index funds offer DRIPs with no transaction fees or commissions, making it a low-cost option to grow your portfolio. Check your brokerage to confirm if this method is available.

THE GROWTH OF SMALL INVESTMENTS

Let's say you can invest either $50 or $100 each month. The chart shows how much your investments will grow in 40 years.

If you choose to invest $50 each month, it will grow to $132,821.81. However, by adding an extra $50 each month, your portfolio grows to $265,643.62. That's more than $130,000, with just an additional $24,000 invested.

In time, start increasing the amount you can invest to accelerate towards your goals.

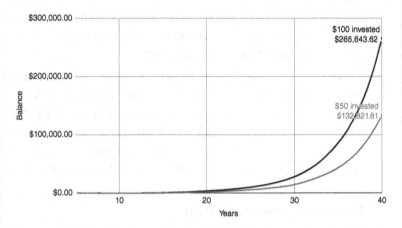

This example is for illustrative purposes only, assuming a moderate 7% return rate on your stock market investments. The historic annualized average return of the S&P 500 is around 10.5% since its inception in 1957.

Source: Adapted from https://www.spglobal.com/.

HOW TO OWN SHARES OF YOUR EMPLOYER'S STOCK

In the Earn Money pillar, you learned the importance of using your benefits to calculate your total earnings. Many publicly traded companies offer an employee benefit to become a stockholder. It's an opportunity to accelerate reaching your retirement and financial independence goals by using stock-related benefits. They include:

Employee Stock Purchase Plans (ESPPs)

ESPPs are programs where employees can buy company stock at a discounted price, usually through payroll deductions. The benefits of ESPPs are:

- **Discounted Stock:** You get to purchase company shares at a lower price than what the general public pays.
- **Regular Contributions:** You can contribute a portion of your salary regularly towards buying stocks, making it easier to build up ownership in the company.
- **Potential Profit:** If the stock price rises, you can sell your shares at a higher market value and potentially make a profit.

Employee Stock Options

Employee stock options give employees the right to buy company shares at a pre-determined price, known as the "strike price." The benefits of stock options are:

- **Low Initial Cost:** You don't have to buy the stock immediately; you can purchase it later at the agreed-upon price.
- **Potential for Gains:** If the stock price rises above the strike price, you can exercise the options, buy the stock at the lower price, and then sell it at the higher market price, making a profit.

Restricted Stock Units (RSUs)

RSUs are grants of company stock given to employees, but they are not immediately transferable. The benefits of RSUs are:

- **Company Ownership:** RSUs give you ownership shares in the company, even though you can't sell them right away.
- **Vesting Period:** Over time, RSUs "vest," meaning they become fully transferable. Once they vest, you can sell the shares or hold on to them as you see fit.

Other ways to get stocks from publicly traded companies you work for include:

- **Stock Grants:** Some companies may give employees outright stock grants as part of their compensation package.

(Continued)

(Continued)

- **Employee Stock Ownership Programs (ESOPs):** Similar to ESPPs, ESOPs allow employees to buy shares of the company, often with contributions from the employer.
- **Stock Bonuses:** In some cases, companies may offer stock bonuses as rewards for exceptional performance.

Participating in these stock-related benefits is a great way to contribute to your retirement goals and financial independence.

TAKE ACTION

Use the worksheet in the Appendix to complete the exercises:

1. Calculate your financial independence number.
2. Determine how much you need.
3. Open your brokerage account.
4. Make your first investment.
5. Learn whether your company offers stock options or stock purchase plans.

 Invest for Independence Recap

In this lesson, you mastered how the stock market works and the steps needed to invest for independence, from calculating your FI number to automating your investing. You've gained the knowledge to determine what type of brokerage account to open and learned about index funds and ETFs as an investing strategy.

The chapter explored these six steps:

- **Step 1:** Starting with investing fundamentals
- **Step 2:** Calculating your financial independence number
- **Step 3:** Determining how much to invest
- **Step 4:** Opening a brokerage account
- **Step 5:** Choosing an investment activity
- **Step 6:** Automating your investing

You don't have to wait for traditional retirement to live your dream life. You can regain your time freedom much sooner by intentionally investing with the goal of reaching financial independence.

GROW MONEY SUMMARY

Congratulations, you've finished the Grow Money pillar.

You are an investor. You're making your money smile by giving it a job through investing, which makes your money grow.

In this pillar, you learned the skills to earn more on savings and contribute strategically to retirement accounts. And you took the first step towards financial independence. You also gained the knowledge to keep things simple by building your portfolio of low-cost index funds. The lessons you mastered were:

- **Lesson 1:** Build Your Investments
- **Lesson 2:** Contribute to Your Retirement
- **Lesson 3:** Invest for Independence

The key messages are to start investing, start small, stay consistent, and think long term.

In the next pillar, you'll learn about enhancing credit scores, using leverage, and getting rid of debt forever through the Borrow Money lessons.

PILLAR **IV**

Borrow Money

*C*redit Strategy

You can use other people's money to achieve your goals. It's called borrowing, financing, or using credit.

Credit is like money's cousin—closely related. Both money and credit are financial tools, but they aren't the same thing. While your money can be used as you wish, credit comes with the responsibility of borrowing someone else's money. It must be repaid.

Although some experts argue against credit, claiming that it only leads to distress, they often overlook the fact that credit can also push you forward. It enables you to achieve many life goals if used wisely. The key word is *wisely*.

In these lessons, you'll learn how to use credit as leverage to build wealth strategically.

Borrow Money	*Use credit as leverage to build wealth.*

It's important to emphasize that uncontrolled credit use often leads to long-term debt. And debt is a ball and chain that keeps you from taking leaps into your ideal future. The more you owe, the less freedom you actually have. However, my main objective is to not discourage you from using credit altogether. The goal is using credit only in a way that benefits your overall financial well-being.

With that said, I want to acknowledge those who may be overburdened by debt. If your debt is causing stress and affecting your health, the priority should be to free yourself from that burden. And you'll learn how to do just that in this pillar.

The fourth pillar is Borrow Money—your credit strategy. In the Borrow Money pillar, you'll learn to distinguish the differences between access to credit and being in debt. The following lessons are:

- **Lesson 1:** Use Your Leverage
- **Lesson 2:** Enhance Your Credit Report and Credit Score
- **Lesson 3:** Eliminate Your Debt

Let's get borrowing!

CHAPTER **10**

Use Your Leverage

Before diving in, let's do a credit assessment.

What's your relationship with credit? How are you using it? Do you think of credit as a means to get things or a tool to build a life? Did the last thing you financed add to your net worth? Is your debt keeping you up at night?

Think thoroughly about these questions. Jot down your thoughts. And take your time.

The reality is such that for some, managing credit is a healthy and positive experience, while it can be stressful and challenging for others. Here's the thing about credit and debt. We associate a lot of emotions with them. We feel worthy when others extend credit to us and feel shame and guilt when we carry too much debt. Shifting your mindset around credit and debt is vital to your financial well-being.

In this chapter, you'll learn to shift your credit mindset and understand how to use debt as leverage.

- **Step 1:** Understanding your credit use
- **Step 2:** Financing your purchases

■ **Step 3:** Building your credit profile

■ **Step 4:** Using your credit as leverage

STEP 1: UNDERSTANDING YOUR CREDIT USE

You've probably heard about "good" or "bad" debt. And you might have wondered what that actually means. The truth is that debt is neither good nor bad. It's simply the result of using credit. How debt supports your life goals is one story. How that debt makes you feel is another.

The Good, the Bad, and the Cred-Ugly

Credit can do good. Credit can be used badly. And credit turned into unmanageable debt is cred-ugly.

"It's concerning when people talk negatively about credit because there are not many people who can, for instance, buy a home without debt," says Saundra Davis, creator of the Financial Fitness Coach (FFC®) certification program. "Credit isn't inherently bad," Saundra adds.

I couldn't agree more. During our conversation, I shared how my travels across the globe showed me the benefits of credit. In places where credit access is limited, there's little economic mobility. And in countries like the United States, where credit can be granted with a signature, it has allowed many to move up the socioeconomic ladder.

Take me as an example. I would not have been able to afford life-changing choices without credit access. For instance, student loans get a bad rap. However, this form of credit allowed me to afford college, fulfilling the American dream instilled by my parents. The college education, for both undergrad and graduate degrees, helped my professional aspirations and supported my upward mobility. I used credit to achieve life goals, contributing to my financial success.

"Debt is leverage and the issue is when we use it to live a lifestyle way above our means," said Saundra.

Unfortunately, I used credit badly too and relied on credit cards to keep a lifestyle I couldn't afford. Admittedly, I was cred-ugly, amassing tens of thousands in consumer debt that affected my mental and emotional health. But I eventually learned to manage credit. The knowledge of how to borrow better was a game-changer. There is a better way to borrow money.

So what are the differences between "good," "bad," and "cred-ugly" debt?

Examples of "Good" Debt

Good debt is typically associated with credit use that leads to a positive change in net worth. For example, a mortgage helps you purchase a home that eventually appreciates in value, taking student loans to get a degree can lead to a higher-income career, and borrowing can help you start a small profitable business. Think of good debt as a way to use other people's money to purchase assets or give you access to wealth-creating opportunities.

Examples of "Bad" Debt

Bad debt is associated with financing purchases that have no positive impact on net worth. It's using credit to pay for lifestyle expenses. For example, you have a loan for a car that's above your means, straining your finances. It's important to know that a car is a depreciating asset, often losing a percentage of its value as soon as it's driven off the dealership lot.

Another example is using credit to finance a vacation, souring the memories because of the remaining debt. Or using credit to keep up appearances and impress people you don't necessarily care about. It's also using credit to buy things to cope with uncomfortable situations and emotions.

When you buy more than you can afford, buy more than you need, or finance more than what's necessary, it compounds financial issues. Essentially, bad debt is buying things for more than they're worth.

Examples of the Cred-Ugly

Credit becomes really ugly when it turns into long-term debt and affects your mood and attitude towards life. Most people with debt feel a greater amount of stress. You might feel depressed, anxious, frustrated, and exhausted thinking about debt. It can be really debilitating.

Debt is that burden on your shoulders or the weight you feel on your chest. It pushes you down and keeps you from making the life changes you want. It can easily trap you in a job you hate because you simply need income to pay the debt.

But credit doesn't have to turn ugly.

Using credit for purchases with long-term positive impact is crucial. If you're going to owe money to someone or a company, it might as well be debt that adds to your net worth and improves your financial health.

STEP 2: FINANCING YOUR PURCHASES

How much do you know about financing?

Credit is a financial tool that lets you borrow money or get stuff without paying all at once. It can help you reach life milestones and do important things you might not be able to afford upfront.

Your Available Financing Options

Different places like banks, credit unions, online lenders, and alternative financing companies offer this tool in different forms. Some are better than others for specific purchases. Choosing the right financing for your situation is essential.

Credit Cards

Your first relationship with credit may be through a credit card. It's a form of financing that offers cardholders access to a revolving line of credit. When a credit card is used to make a purchase, you'll receive a monthly statement with a minimum payment and due date. If you do not pay the entire balance in full, you'll begin to accrue interest on the remaining unpaid balance.

Credit cards are issued with a credit limit, enabling you to make purchases up to the limit. Some offer purchase protection, warranty extensions, and rewards points. Credit card issuers offer different terms, interest rates, fees, and benefits. You have many options to choose from.

Lines of Credit

This works like a credit card without the card. A line of credit is a pre-approved loan authorization with a specific borrowing limit based on creditworthiness. A line of credit allows you to obtain many loans without reapplying each time. If the total of borrowed money does not exceed the credit limit, you're good to go. Lines of credit can be secured, such as a home equity line of credit, or unsecured, like a personal line of credit.

FINANCING COMES IN DIFFERENT FORMS

Unsecured and Secured

Loans fall into one of two categories: secured and unsecured.

- **Secured loans require collateral.** They're tied to an asset that can be seized and sold in case of loan default. These loans are auto loans tied to a vehicle, home loans to a house, and personal loans to a savings account. Interest rates are usually lower compared to unsecured loans.
- **Unsecured loans require no collateral.** Lenders will approve unsecured loans based on income, credit history, and credit score. Your interest rate usually depends on your credit score, with the best rates for those deemed lower risk. Examples of unsecured loans include personal loans, debt consolidation loans, student loans, and any-purpose loans.

Fixed or Variable Rate

Loans can have a fixed rate or variable rate. For a **fixed-rate loan**, the rate and payments stay the same until the term and balance are paid off. **Variable loans** have rates that rise and fall based on the market conditions of the index to which they are tied, but fluctuations are usually capped.

Common Loan Types

Installment loans refer to borrowing a fixed amount of money at once and repaying the loan over a set number of payments, referred to as installments. The most common are home, student, auto, and personal loans.

	Loan Description	Typical Term Length	Secured or Unsecured	Fixed or Variable Rates
Home Loans	For home purchases (mortgage or home equity loans)	15 or 30 years	Secured	Fixed and Variable
Student Loans	For higher education purposes (federal and private student loans)	Varies	Unsecured	Fixed and Variable
Auto Loans	For vehicle purchases (cars, RVs, motorcycles)	Up to 8 years	Secured	Fixed
Personal Loans	For any purpose (big ticket items and debt consolidation)	Varies	Unsecured	Fixed and Variable

Home Loans

Mortgages are used to purchase homes. They make affording a home possible by spreading the cost of a large purchase over many years. The most common mortgage term is 15 to 30 years. The mortgage is paid in fixed monthly installments.

A home equity loan or a second mortgage is a loan that places a security interest on the home. It can be used for home remodeling or any other purpose. Since the loan is collateralized with the home, the interest rates are lower than a personal loan.

It's important to know that unpaid mortgages and equity loans can lead to foreclosure, a legal process allowing a lender to take ownership of the home for failure to make payments.

Student Loans

Federal student loans are either subsidized or unsubsidized and have fixed or variable interest rates. The benefits include deferred payments (no payment required while enrolled at least part-time), student loan forgiveness, and loan repayment plans. **Federal unsubsidized loans** are available for most borrowers regardless of financial needs. In comparison, **federal subsidized loans** are offered to students with the highest financial needs. There are federal caps on the number of student loans you can take.

Private student loans are offered by private lenders (banks and financing companies), requiring underwriting and considering income, credit history, and cosigners for approval. Interest rates can be fixed or variable and loan amounts are based on your financial situation. Unlike federal loans, private loans might require payments while in school.

Additionally, **student loan refinancing** is an option to turn multiple private loans into one loan, making it easier to manage and repay. You can include federal loans in a student loan refinance, but before doing so, consider the federal benefits you may lose by refinancing them. Alternatively, you can consolidate all federal loans through the federal consolidation loan program.

Personal Loans

Lenders market personal loans under various names, yet fundamentally they serve the same purpose. These loans can fund your personal needs—whether purchasing a car, covering wedding expenses, consolidating credit card debt, funding a vacation, or acquiring high-priced appliances. Terms for personal loans depend on the lender and can vary greatly. The actual loan amounts and interest rates might be influenced by factors such as your income, credit history, and debt-to-income ratio.

Auto Loans

An auto loan is linked to a specific vehicle. This type of loan is for financing a new or used vehicle or refinancing existing ones. Actual terms and conditions of the loans vary based on the lender. And the duration of auto loans can range from 24 to 84 months. Since the loan is collateralized with the car, it can be repossessed by the lender if payments are not made.

In addition to the loan options I've explained, many lenders provide specialized loans tailored to specific purchases, such as financing a motorcycle, RV, boat, watercraft, and more. Some financing companies might even offer loans to address immediate cash needs, such as payday loans. However, these loans typically have higher interest rates and fees, making them less desirable.

Financing Stuff at the Store

Retail store financing, also known as retail financing or store credit, refers to financing offered by retailers for use in their stores, allowing customers to make purchases without paying the full amount upfront. This type of financing is commonly used for big-ticket items like appliances, electronics, furniture, jewelry, and even healthcare services.

You might have seen retail stores advertise 0% financing for 12 months. This lets you purchase an item that day and pay in full within 12 months. It's a good option. However, if you don't pay the financed amount in the agreed terms, you may incur the accrued interest charges for the entire 12 months.

Be mindful and fully understand the financing terms, including interest rates, fees, and potential penalties for missed payments and remaining balances.

WHAT'S THE TOTAL COST OF BORROWING?

A "good" debt can become a "bad" debt if you're unaware of the total cost of borrowing. The less you know, the more you'll pay. The factors below determine how much it costs to borrow money. It's crucial to know them.

Loan Amount	Borrow only what you need. Even if you qualify for a higher loan amount, be careful of overextending yourself. The less money you borrow, the less you'll have to repay.
Interest Rate	The APR you qualify for is based on your credit history. The stronger your credit score, the better APR from the lender. A better rate means a lower cost.

Term	Keep an eye on the length of time to repay the loan. The longer the term, the more it will cost you. Fortunately, most loans allow you to pay more than your scheduled monthly payment.
Fees	Check for additional fees that can increase the total cost of financing.

How Loan Terms Impact the Total Cost of Borrowing

Many financing companies will focus on monthly payments, not the total cost, to determine what you can afford. Simply focusing on the monthly payment can turn an otherwise good purchase into bad debt.

Let's use a common reason for borrowing money: financing a car.

Compare a $25,000 car loan at a 5.00% interest rate across different loan terms. You can finance a car to get a lower monthly payment but end up with a higher total cost of borrowing.

Loan Term	Monthly Payment	Total Interest Paid
36 months (3 years)	$749	$1,974
60 months (5 years)	$472	$3,307

How Interest Rates Affect the Total Cost of Borrowing

Using the car example, let's compare a $25,000 car loan financed for 60 months at two different interest rates: 5% and 7%. You'll notice that the higher the interest rates, the more you pay for the same purchase.

Loan Term	Interest Rate	Monthly Payment	Total Interest Paid
60 months (5 years)	5%	$472	$3,307
60 months (5 years)	7%	$495	$4,702

Choosing the right lender, the best product, the lowest rate, and the shorter term is a financially healthy move.

In the next step, you'll learn how credit impacts other parts of your life and why you must build your credit profile.

STEP 3: BUILDING YOUR CREDIT PROFILE

A credit profile is a personal record of your borrowing and repayment activity. It's what is often referred to as a credit report that shows how you're managing credit accounts, such as loans and credit cards. The lenders report the history to credit bureaus that maintain the record.

Why is it important to have a credit profile?

There is a good chance that in the future, you'll want to finance a purchase or need a credit card for travel or a loan for an emergency. With credit history, you'll have better odds of getting approved, won't need a cosigner, will qualify for lower interest rates, and will receive better terms such as no security deposit or lower downpayments.

However, having credit doesn't mean being indebted. You can use credit and don't have to carry debt. For instance, using a credit card and paying off the balance in full each month is one way to maintain a positive credit history without paying interest.

You might not want to use credit, but not having a credit profile can hurt you.

Your credit history can be used for renting an apartment, turning on utilities, getting internet access, or activating cell service. It can also be utilized for employment opportunities, security clearances, and professional licenses and used to determine auto insurance premiums. Having no credit history makes living a bit more challenging.

HOW CREDIT AFFECTS OTHER PARTS OF YOUR LIFE

1. Renting an apartment or leasing a home

You may find yourself renting if you can't qualify for a mortgage. If that is the case, credit carries weight in the rental world, too. Many landlords will request a copy of your credit report to determine your ability to repay monthly obligations. Having a poor or no credit history can keep you from renting a nice apartment and could mean a larger security deposit or require a cosigner.

2. Getting utilities, cell plans, internet, and cable service

Credit matters when it comes to securing basic utilities such as water, gas, and electricity. This also applies to cellular plans. The providers will run a credit check and determine if a security deposit is required.

3. Applying for auto insurance

Many auto insurance providers use credit history to determine your premiums. You might find yourself having higher premiums and larger monthly payments. It might not seem fair, but having a history of late payments may lead the insurance provider to deem you a greater risk.

4. Getting a job offer

Some employers run credit checks to determine your suitability for a job. For example, finance or law enforcement careers might require applicants to have good credit or lower debt obligations. An employer who uses credit history as part of the vetting process can only use the information found on "employment-specific" credit reports. They also cannot use credit scores to deny an applicant.

If you've never had credit under your name or if you have a limited credit history, you may hear the terms "no credit file" or "thin credit file." Consumers with thin or limited credit files may not have enough information to produce a credit score, which can affect an approval decision.

How to Build Your Credit Profile

It's possible you can apply for financing and get approved by a lender, thus helping to establish your credit history. And it's equally possible you'll get turned down because you lack credit history. If the latter is the case, and you're starting your credit journey or need to rebuild your credit, follow the advice in the next sections.

Get a Secured Credit Card

A secured credit card works like a regular (unsecured) credit card, except it requires a security deposit. For example, a $500 deposit gives you access to a $500 credit limit. Many financial institutions offer secured credit cards. Stay away from secured credit cards with application fees, annual fees, and monthly service charges. You have better options, like secured cards from credit unions. They offer some of the best interest rates and terms. Inquire with them on how to apply.

Get a Department or Retail Store Card

Many retailers offer their own branded credit cards. You'll notice these cards don't have the Visa or Mastercard logos, and they can only be used at a specific retailer or store. Some retail store cards have easier approval terms. The credit limits tend to be lower, such as $100, but can still establish your credit. Remember, you create a positive repayment history by using the store card and paying the balance in full each month.

Get a Secured Personal Loan

Many banks and credit unions offer secured loans requiring a security deposit into a savings account. Your loan amount is based on the security deposit amount. Once the loan is paid off, you can access your security deposit. It's wise to automate your payments so you don't miss them. Also, having an unsecured personal loan can add to your credit mix and payment history, improving your credit score.

Get a Credit Builder Account

Some alternative financing companies (and a growing number of banks and credit unions) offer credit builder accounts to establish or rebuild your credit. They don't use credit history in the approval process. It works like this. After identity verification, they'll open a savings account and approve a loan for a small amount. The approved loan is deposited into that savings account. You're required to make repayments based on the terms outlined. For instance, a $1,000 credit builder loan has repayment terms of $85 a month for the next 12 months. Make the payments on time and this will be reported to the credit bureaus. Your loan payments, minus any fees and interest owed, will equal the amount borrowed. After the term, you'll get access to your $1000 savings plus any interest earned.

Get a Friend and Become an Authorized User

If you know someone with good credit, this option is viable. Becoming an authorized user means you'll get that card's credit history added to your report. Unlike that of a cosigner or co-borrower, you aren't responsible for the debt payments as an authorized user. However, late payments or large balances on the card you're authorized on negatively affect you. Here are two more things to know: 1) You don't actually need to have the physical card or use that credit card, and 2) some creditors don't report authorized users to the credit bureaus, so you'll need to check with the card issuer.

Establishing a good credit history supports your financial health. And using credit responsibly can help you build your wealth.

STEP 4: USING YOUR CREDIT AS LEVERAGE

"Stay away from credit" is a motto some financial experts tout as the key to wealth. After studying these people, I learned how they've used credit as leverage in the past to build their assets. Now, I totally understand why they want others to stay away from credit: it can lead to unmanageable debt and a lot of stress.

As someone who's experienced extreme credit distress and broken free from the debt ball and chain, I have a different take. Sure, I don't want you using credit for the sake of buying stuff to fill a void in your life. I want you to use credit to build a life. Here's how you can make it work for you.

Buying Assets That Can Grow in Value

Credit can help you buy things that might be worth more later. For example, you could borrow money to buy a house or invest in a business. As time goes by, the value of these things can go up and improve your net worth—the financial number that shows how much you own (assets) after subtracting what you owe (liabilities).

FINANCING AN ASSET

For example, let's say you want to buy a house. You can save up the full price (which might take a while) or get a mortgage. If the house costs $300,000 and you put down $60,000 (20%) as a downpayment, you'd need a mortgage for the remaining $240,000.

Here's what happened: Let's assume your house appreciates (increases in value) by 4% yearly. After a year, your house is now worth $312,000.

Impact on your net worth:

Initial Net Worth:

- House Value: $300,000
- Mortgage: $240,000
- Your Initial Net Worth: House Value − Mortgage = $300,000 − $240,000 = $60,000

After a Year:

- House Value: $312,000
- Mortgage: Still $240,000 (You're making regular payments)
- Your New Net Worth: House Value − Mortgage = $312,000 − $240,000 = $72,000

Lesson: Even though you owe money (the mortgage), your net worth increased. By using the mortgage to buy an asset that appreciates in value, you've actually made more money than you owe. This is called leverage—using a small amount of your own money to control a larger asset. As time passes, your net worth can keep growing, thanks to the house's value going up.

Learning and Earning More

You can use credit to invest in learning new things, like going to college, taking courses, getting training, or for a certification. With more knowledge, you might be able to find a better job or start a business that makes more money. This can help you grow your savings and net worth over time.

FINANCING AN EDUCATION

Taking out student loans can be a strategic investment in your future, leading to a promising return on investment (ROI).

Imagine you're considering two paths after high school: attending college or entering the workforce directly. You decide to pursue a college degree that costs $50,000 in tuition and expenses over four years. To cover these costs, you take out student loans with an average interest rate of 5%.

Here's what happened: Upon graduating, you secure a job with a starting salary of $50,000, while your friend who entered the workforce earns $30,000 annually. Over the next 20 years, your salary increases by an average of 3% annually, while your friend's salary remains constant.

Calculating the ROI:

Total Earnings:

- Your Total Earnings = Starting Salary + Salary Increases Over 20 Years
- Your Total Earnings = $50,000 + ($50,000 x 0.03 x 20) = $2,100,000
- Your Friend's Total Earnings = Starting Salary x 20 Years
- Your Friend's Total Earnings = $30,000 x 20 = $600,000

Total Loan Payments:

- Total Loan Payments = Loan Amount x (1 + Interest Rate)^Number of Years
- Total Loan Payments = $50,000 x (1 + 0.05)^20 = $132,677

Net Earnings after Loan Repayment:

- Your Net Earnings = Your Total Earnings − Total Loan Payments
- Your Net Earnings = $2,100,000 − $132,677 = $1,967,323

(Continued)

(*Continued*)

Lesson: Your decision to borrow for college has resulted in a substantial return on investment. Despite the loan repayment, your net earnings over 20 years amount to $1,967,323, while your friend's earnings remain at $600,000. This difference highlights how investing in a college education can lead to higher lifetime earnings that can then be used to purchase assets.

The ROI on education varies based on factors like a chosen career, salary growth, and loan terms. Borrowing for college can lead to a good return, but it's vital to borrow wisely. Do your research to determine how education investment contributes to higher earnings.

Growing Money Through Debt Management

Sometimes, borrowing a little money can be better than spending all your savings. For instance, instead of using all your savings to make a large purchase, you could use credit to spread out the payments. This way, your savings can remain invested and potentially earn a return while you manage your debt responsibly.

USING LEVERAGE TO GROW MONEY

A popular debate is whether to pay off your mortgage early or invest the money in the stock market instead. The real answer is that it depends on your situation. Having a mortgage-free house may give you peace of mind. However, investing the money instead may lead to higher returns.

The scenario: Should you pay off your 30-year mortgage early or invest your extra money in the stock market? Both do come with different risks and rewards. Let's break it down using a simple example.

Option 1: Paying off Your Mortgage Early

Imagine you have a 30-year mortgage with a remaining balance of $150,000 and an interest rate of 4%. You can make an extra payment of $10,000 towards your mortgage. By doing so, you'll reduce your outstanding balance to $140,000.

Pros:

- Paying off your mortgage gives you a guaranteed return, as you'll save on interest payments over the loan's remaining term.
- Owning your home outright can provide a sense of security and reduce financial stress.

Cons:

- While paying off your mortgage is a safe option, you might miss out on potentially higher returns in the stock market.

Option 2: Investing in the Stock Market

Alternatively, you could invest $10,000 in the stock market. Historically, the stock market has generated an average annual return of around 7% after adjusting for inflation. (Learn more about investing in the Grow Money pillar.)

Pros:

- Investing in the stock market could yield higher long-term returns than the interest savings from paying off your mortgage.
- Stock market investments allow you to diversify your portfolio, potentially spreading risk and increasing your chances of growing your money.

Cons:

- The stock market can be volatile, and there's a chance you could lose money, especially in the short term.

What's the right choice? Choosing between paying off your mortgage early and investing in stocks ultimately depends on your financial goals and risk tolerance. Paying off your mortgage could be a better move if you prioritize the peace of mind that comes with owning your home outright and want a guaranteed return.

On the other hand, investing in the stock market might be more appealing if you're comfortable with some risk and seek potentially higher returns. Keep in mind that the stock market can be unpredictable, and there's a chance your investments could temporarily decrease in value.

Ultimately, it's possible to strike a balance between the two options. You might decide to make extra mortgage payments while contributing to your investment portfolio.

Don't let credit run your life. Manage credit and use it as leverage to help grow wealth over time.

TAKE ACTION

1. Complete the credit assessment found in the Appendix.

 Use Your Leverage Recap

You don't have to finance purchases, but credit is necessary in the world we live in. Knowing how to manage credit is vital to your financial well-being.

In this chapter, you learned all about financing and using credit. You gained knowledge on building wealth through leverage, and on how to borrow money that supports your long-term goals.

The lessons explained these steps:

- **Step 1:** Understanding your credit use
- **Step 2:** Financing your purchases
- **Step 3:** Building your credit profile
- **Step 4:** Using your credit as leverage

Another congrats is in order. You've finished the lessons to use credit as a tool and debt as leverage. In the next chapter, you'll learn everything you need to know about credit reports and credit scores.

CHAPTER 11

Enhance Your Credit Report and Scores

You have more control over your credit report and scores than you're led to believe. It's a matter of understanding how it all works and learning the many ways you can positively affect your credit history.

Let's start with the basics.

What is a credit report? It's a file that contains personal information such as your name, address, list of employers, credit inquiries, and the history and status of your credit accounts. The account information includes your payment history, number of credit accounts, credit limits, credit used, and any collection accounts. This information is collected by private companies referred to as **credit bureaus**.

A credit bureau's main function is to track and report your credit, including your history of paying bills. They may also calculate your ability to repay future loans (e.g., credit scores). Credit bureaus offer two services:

1. They compile credit histories on prospective borrowers.
2. They provide credit reports to lenders.

The three major credit bureaus in the United States are Experian, TransUnion, and Equifax.

It's worth repeating that credit bureaus are private companies, not government agencies. The bureaus are regulated and must follow federal and state laws.

In this chapter, you'll learn the elements of a credit report, where to get your free credit report and credit score, and how to correct inaccuracies and improve scores. The lessons present the following six steps:

- **Step 1:** Requesting your credit report
- **Step 2:** Reviewing your credit report
- **Step 3:** Disputing credit report inaccuracies
- **Step 4:** Getting your credit score
- **Step 5:** Improving your credit score
- **Step 6:** Monitoring your credit

STEP 1: REQUESTING YOUR CREDIT REPORT

The Fair Credit Reporting Act (FCRA) is a federal law that gives you the right to see your credit records and correct any mistakes. It requires each nationwide credit reporting company—Experian, TransUnion, and Equifax—to provide you with a free copy of your credit report, at your request, once every 12 months. Accessing your report online requires entering personal information and passing identity verification.

THREE WAYS TO REQUEST YOUR FREE CREDIT REPORT

To comply with the FCRA, the three major credit bureaus have set up one website, a toll-free telephone number, and a mailing address through which you can order your free annual report.

Choose one of the following to order your free copy:

- Visit AnnualCreditReport.com (the quickest way)
- Call 1-877-322-8228
- Complete an Annual Credit Report Request Form and mail it to:

  Annual Credit Report Request Service
  P.O. Box 105281
  Atlanta, GA 30348-5281

If you've already obtained your free annual reports and need additional copies or more frequent access, you can request them directly from the credit bureau's website. They offer one-time access for a fee and various subscription plans, including monthly credit reports and monitoring services.

Credit Bureau	Website	Telephone
Experian	www.experian.com	(888) 397-3742
TransUnion	www.transunion.com	(800) 916-8800
Equifax	www.equifax.com	(866) 349-5191

Additionally, some authorized third-party services provide credit monitoring and credit report access. You've probably seen these companies advertising their services either as a freemium or a paid service. I do want you to make sure that the service you choose is legitimate and reputable before providing any personal information. For updated resources on the best credit report monitoring service, visit thesmilemoney.com/book.

TIPS ON REQUESTING AND REVIEWING YOUR CREDIT REPORT

It might be tempting to request all three credit reports at once. Don't do that! You might get overwhelmed. Instead, request one report at a time. Follow these simple steps:

(Continued)

(*Continued*)

1. Choose one credit bureau to start with and request your credit report.

2. Review and verify the information and take notes of inaccuracies.

3. Dispute inaccurate information directly with that credit bureau and wait for the resolution.

4. Request a report from another credit bureau, and repeat the process until you've received, reviewed, verified, and corrected the information on all three bureaus.

STEP 2: REVIEWING YOUR CREDIT REPORT

Credit bureaus do their best to ensure the data reported is accurate, but it's very common that credit reports can have incorrect information. Although credit bureaus are mandated by law to report only accurate information, it's up to you to verify the accuracy of what's reported.

Let's review the five sections that make up your credit report.

Section 1: Personal Information

This section includes your personal information, such as your name, Social Security number, and date of birth. It will also list your current and previous addresses and phone numbers. Additionally, this section will show current and previous employers.

Section 2: Inquiries

The inquiry section lists companies that accessed your credit report. It includes companies that received your information to offer credit, provide a service, or for employment.

There are two types of inquiries: hard and soft. The type of inquiry impacts your credit score differently. When you apply for credit or a service, it's considered a hard inquiry, and it's added to your credit report. Hard inquiries are viewable by others and can impact your credit score. Some lenders perform a soft inquiry using just your name and address to see if you prequalify for a loan. Soft inquiries are only viewable by you and do not impact your credit score.

Section 3: Collection Items

The collection section lists unpaid debts sold or transferred from the original creditor to a collection agency. A collection agency is a private company whose business model is centered on buying debt from creditors and getting the borrower to repay the balanced owed to them. If you're getting calls from collection agents, their information will be found in this section.

Section 4: Public Records

The public records section lists bankruptcies. Due to recent federal regulations, it no longer includes liens, civil suits, and judgments.

Section 5: Credit Accounts

The credit section details your relationship with creditors. It includes the start date of the credit, type of credit (credit card, mortgage, loan), the history of payments, account status, and credit limits or loan amount. The accounts appearing in your report are referred to as tradelines. For example, a car loan and credit card found on your credit report would be considered two tradelines.

What to Look for in Your Credit Report

Credit reports display only your credit relationships. It does *not* include the following:

- Race
- Religion
- Political party affiliation
- Medical history
- Lifestyle
- Background
- Criminal record

I want you to carefully examine your report for any discrepancies. Review the sections and look for inaccuracies in personal information, accounts, payment history, and any unfamiliar or suspicious entries.

Credit Report Verification Checklist*	
Credit Report Section	**Description**
Personal Information	Verify your name, Social Security, date of birth, current and previous addresses, and phone numbers.
Employer Information	Verify current and previous employers.
Credit Accounts	Verify account status (closed, opened), creditor names, date opened, credit limits, balances, and payment history.
Inquiries	Review the soft and hard inquiries. Verify that hard inquiries are from your attempts to acquire credit.
Collection Items	Verify for any outstanding collection reported.
Public Records	Verify public records are reported correctly. It should only show bankruptcy if it applies to your situation.

*See Appendix for the Credit Report Verification Worksheet.

The information found in your credit report is provided by furnishers, including:

- Banks and credit unions
- Finance companies
- Student loans and loan servicers
- Mortgage companies
- Collection agencies
- State and federal courts

If there are furnishers you don't recognize or information provided by them that's inaccurate, start the dispute process. You'll learn how to do that in the next step.

It's worth reminding that you should thoroughly and carefully examine each section. As you review your report, use a highlighter to mark and identify discrepancies. On a separate sheet, document the errors you're seeing. Use the worksheet in the Appendix to assist you.

ARE YOU A VICTIM OF IDENTITY THEFT?

Identity theft is when your personal information—name or Social Security number—is used to commit fraud, such as opening new credit accounts, applying for loans, and receiving benefits.

After reviewing your credit report, you might have discovered information unknown to you. It's possible your identity has been used fraudulently. Here are two things to do immediately:

Place a fraud alert

A fraud alert requires creditors who check your credit report to take steps to verify your identity before doing any of the following: opening a new account, issuing an additional card, or increasing the credit limit on an existing account based on a consumer's request. When you place a fraud alert on your credit report with one of the credit bureaus, it must notify the others.

Place a security freeze

A security freeze or credit freeze is designed to prevent credit bureaus from releasing your credit report without your implicit consent. This prevents new creditors from accessing your credit file and opening accounts in your name until the freeze is removed. You can place a credit freeze on your credit file anytime, but you must contact each credit bureau.

STEP 3: DISPUTING CREDIT REPORT ERRORS

Federal law protects your rights to accurate information on credit reports. However, it's up to you to review the reports and initiate the dispute of inaccuracies. You can easily submit disputes online through the credit bureau websites. And it's best to submit your initial dispute with detailed information and include any documents.

The credit bureaus are legally required to investigate your claim whenever you dispute a record. They'll forward all documents to the furnisher (the creditor or company reporting the information) and report the results to you. Credit bureaus have 30 days from receipt of the dispute to provide an answer and may respond with the following:

- **Frivolous:** If the credit bureau determines that your dispute is frivolous, it can choose not to investigate the dispute. They must send you a notice within five days saying they have made that decision.
- **Correction:** If the furnisher agrees with your dispute and fixes the error, it must notify the credit bureaus to update their reports with the correct information.
- **Accurate:** If the furnisher determines the information is accurate, they'll inform the credit bureau, and it will remain in your report.

If you disagree with the results, you can request a reevaluation by submitting additional information that supports your claim to the credit bureaus. You can also reach out to the data furnisher directly and request corrections. It's crucial you explain the situation and share any supporting documents and notes with them.

Additionally, you can add a brief statement on your credit report explaining your side of the story regarding disputed records.

In some instances, a credit bureau cannot get a response from the furnisher within the 30-day time frame. This results in the deletion of the record by the credit bureau. However, if the furnisher sends updated information at a later date, the record may reappear.

HOW TO DISPUTE CREDIT REPORT ERRORS

If you find an error on your credit report, dispute the information with the credit bureaus (Experian, TransUnion, and Equifax). Explain in writing what you think is wrong and why it should be corrected. Include copies of documents that support your dispute.

The credit bureaus have made it easy to submit disputes online. However, if you choose to mail a dispute (some recommend doing so), your dispute letter should address the following:

- Supply your contact information, including complete name, address, and telephone number.
- Give the report confirmation number, if available.
- Clearly identify each mistake, such as an account number for any account you may be disputing.
- Explain why you are disputing the information.
- Request that the information be removed or corrected.
- Enclose a copy of the portion of your credit report that contains the disputed items and circle or highlight them. Include copies (not originals) of documents that support your dispute.

Send your letter of dispute to credit bureaus by certified mail with a return receipt. This way you have a record of when the credit bureau received your letter. Here are the contacts for the three nationwide credit bureaus:

Experian

- Online: www.experian.com
- By phone: (888) 397-3742
- By mail: Use the address provided on your credit report or mail your letter to:

Experian
P.O. Box 4500
Allen, TX 75013

TransUnion

- Online: www.transunion.com
- By phone: (800) 916-8800
- By mail: Download the dispute form on the TransUnion website and mail the dispute form with your letter to:

TransUnion LLC
Consumer Dispute Center
P.O. Box 2000
Chester, PA 19016

(*Continued*)

(*Continued*)

Equifax

- Online: www.equifax.com
- By phone: (866) 349-5191
- By mail: Download the dispute form on the Equifax website and mail the dispute form with your letter to:

Equifax Information Services LLC

P.O. Box 740256

Atlanta, GA 30348

Remember to keep copies of your dispute letter and hold on to the original documents. For a sample dispute letter, visit thesmilemoney.com/book.

It might seem like a daunting task to dispute credit report errors, but it is worth the time investment, because the work you do will be reflected in your credit score.

STEP 4: GETTING YOUR CREDIT SCORE

Your credit score is a simple way to assess your credit health. The higher the score, the better you manage credit and debt. It can also mean you experience less financial stress. The most popular credit scores use a range between 300 and 850.

A credit score represents the answer from a mathematical formula that assigns numerical values to information found in your credit report. That's just a fancy way of saying it compiles the information and grades it. Credit scoring companies calculate the three-digit number differently using their own proprietary methods. Because of the different scoring methodologies, you have more than one score.

A few years back, I challenged myself to see how many credit scores I could get. I found 24 different scores. I got my credit scores through the credit bureaus, free credit monitoring services, my credit union, and a few credit cards.

You can have dozens, if not hundreds, of credit score variations. It can get confusing because one company has one score, you have another from a credit monitoring app, and a lender has its own score, too.

What You Really Need to Know about Credit Scores

There are two well-known scoring systems, FICO® and VantageScore. They provide lenders with access to scores using proprietary algorithms. The information used to generate your score is obtained from the credit bureau. So the information in your credit report matters the most.

Many credit monitoring apps and other companies offer educational credit scores. These scores may use a FICO®, VantageScore, or another method to calculate your score using the information found in your credit report. Educational scores focus on helping you understand how you're using credit and provide resources to improve your scores.

And the funny thing about credit scores is that they will increase without you doing anything and decrease through no fault of yours. It's just how the system works: the algorithms are tweaked. It all leads to the ups and downs of your score.

While some people stress about one- or two-point drops, I want you to focus on where your score falls within a range.

Credit Score Ranges

Credit scoring companies and lenders use ranges to assess whether your score is bad or excellent. As a general guideline, determine where your score falls within these ranges.

- Excellent credit: 750+
- Good credit: 700–749
- Fair credit: 650–699
- Poor credit: 600–649
- Bad credit: below 600

The ranges I share are an example, based on my previous experiences working in the financial services industry. Lenders set their own criteria. It is possible that a few points can take you from excellent to good credit or vice versa. Knowing these ranges and where you fall can help you choose the best lender for your situation.

Lenders will modify the credit score ranges to determine the level of risk they are willing to take and set the interest rate based on them.

They also use ranges to make loan decisions systematically—automatic approval, need review, or instant denial.

Credit Score Ranges Example		
Credit Score Ranges	**Interest Rate**	**Results**
Excellent credit: 750+	5%, instant approval	Instant approval
Good credit: 700–749	6%	Approval
Fair credit: 650–699	10%–15%	Approval with review
Poor credit: 600–649	13%–19%	Approval with further review
Bad credit: below 600	–	Not approved

Where Do You Fall in the Credit Score Range?

Start by getting your credit score.

While the Federal Credit Reporting Act (FCRA) established the federal law that guaranteed access to your credit report, it did not require providing free credit scores. You have options, from paid to free versions, either directly with the credit bureaus, through banking relationships, or through a credit monitoring service.

Use the table below to get your free credit scores. Indicate the scoring method and credit bureau used to calculate the score.

Get Your Credit Score			
Source	**Credit Score**	**Credit Bureau** *(Experian, TransUnion, Equifax)*	**Scoring Method** *(FICO®, VantageScore, other)*
Experian. com (example)	748	**Experian**	**FICO®**
Experian.com			
Credit Karma			
Credit Wise			
Other:			

Remember that there are different credit scoring models, and the score you receive may vary depending on the source. It's a good idea to check your credit score from multiple reputable sources to get a comprehensive view of your credit health.

I do want you to be cautious of websites or services that offer free credit scores and trick you into a monthly paid subscription. To find an updated list of paid and free credit score apps, visit thesmilemoney .com/book.

WHERE TO GET YOUR CREDIT SCORE

The good news is there are different ways to get credit scores, including:

- **Credit Bureaus:** The three major credit bureaus—Experian, TransUnion, and Equifax—provide credit scores. You can request your credit score directly from their websites. A fee may apply.
- **Banks, Credit Unions, and Credit Card Companies:** Some financial institutions provide free access to your credit score through their online banking platforms or credit card account dashboards.
- **Credit Monitoring Services:** Many credit monitoring services offer access to your credit score as part of their subscription packages. These services often provide additional benefits like credit monitoring, identity theft protection, and credit report updates.
- **Fintech Apps:** Various financial technology (fintech) apps and platforms offer free access to your credit score as part of their services. These apps might also provide financial insights and recommendations based on your credit profile. These scores are commonly called educational credit scores.
- **Credit Counseling Agencies:** Nonprofit credit counseling agencies may offer free credit counseling services that include reviewing your credit report and score.

STEP 5: IMPROVING YOUR CREDIT SCORE

The first time I reviewed my credit report, I noticed information that did not belong to me. I went through the dispute process to get things fixed, and it led to improved credit scores. I also used tactics to strengthen my score, which you'll learn in this step.

Let's first go over the factors that make up your credit score.

The exact information used by credit scoring providers to calculate your scores is top secret, but there is some publicly available information. FICO®, for instance, has shared its five factors.

1. **Payment history (35%)**

    Your repayment history. It is the largest percentage because paying on time is important for lenders to know.

2. **Amounts owed (30%)**

    Your credit capacity. It's also called credit utilization and is based on the amount of outstanding credit you have against your available credit limits.

3. **Length of credit history (15%)**

    Your time with credit. How long you've had credit plays a role in your credit score. Longer credit histories are viewed positively. By adding new accounts, your average credit history length shortens and this can lower your score.

4. **Types of credit in use (10%)**

    Your use of different types of financing. It's based on a mixture of credit such as credit cards, personal loans, mortgages, and auto loans. Stronger credit scores have a good variety of credit types.

5. **Account inquiries (10%)**

    Your desire for more financing. Applying for credit impacts your credit score. Too many recent loan applications or hard inquiries can have a negative impact.

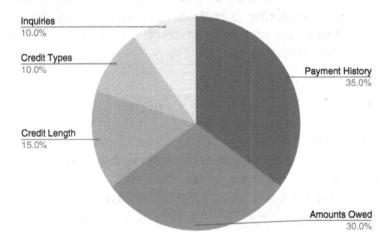

Increasing Your Credit Score

Start by fixing your report and disputing inaccuracies (as you've already read in step 3), and by doing the following:

- **Remove negative tradelines.** If you have negative information on a credit report older than seven years, you can have the information removed. Make sure to keep all positive history in your account.

- **Settle collection accounts.** Contact the collection agency and agree to a settlement of the debt that you can afford to pay today. Request a "pay for delete" and keep records of the name of the person you've been working with, and dates, times, and details of the conversation. If the collection account is not yours, request a "debt verification" letter.

- **Push delinquencies further in time.** If you have a late payment posted on your credit report, make on-time payments and push that delinquency further in the past. Older delinquencies have less impact on your credit score.

To improve other factors used in credit scoring, do the following:

- **Pay bills on time** (payment history). Ensure your bills are all paid on or before the due dates. Late payments have a significant impact on credit scores.

- **Increase your available credit** (amounts owed). Pay down your credit balances. Credit score algorithms look at your available capacity. You can also request a credit limit increase or apply for new credit. Of course, this will only work if you can get approved. Make sure you don't use the new credit line.

- **Keep old accounts open** (credit length). The length of your history matters. It's the average age of all accounts. Having a long history of managing credit impacts scores positively.

- **Avoid opening too many accounts** (inquiries). Each credit application results in a hard inquiry on your credit report, which lowers your score temporarily. Only apply for credit when necessary.

- **Add to the credit mixture** (credit mix). Scoring algorithms look at the types of credit on your file. Adding an installment loan, such as a personal loan, will help boost your score if you have too many credit cards. An excellent way to add a mixture is by opening a secured credit card or secured loan for a small amount and making on-time payments.

- **Become an authorized user** (length, mix, history). Get added as a user on a credit card with a high limit, low balance, and excellent repayment history. Your spouse, partner, best friend, or sibling can help you.

- **Add your rent or utilities** (payment history). Typically, rent and monthly utility payments are not reported. It seems unfair since landlords and utility companies use your credit history. Services are available to report your rent, utility, and cellular service payments. It can give you a credit score boost. Experian, for instance, offers Experian Boost.

HOW AVAILABLE CREDIT IMPACTS YOUR CREDIT SCORE

The credit utilization ratio is linked to the Amounts Owed factor and significantly influences your credit score. This ratio reflects the portion of your available credit that you're presently using. Calculating the ratio involves dividing your overall credit balances by your total credit limits, then multiplying the result by 100 to express it as a percentage.

For example, let's say you have a total credit limit of $10,000 across all your credit cards and lines of credit with a combined balance of $3,000. Your credit utilization would be 30%.

$$(\text{Combined Credit Balances} / \text{Total Credit Limit}) \times 100$$
$$= \text{Credit Utilization Ratio}$$

Combined Credit Balances	Divided By	Total Credit Limit	Multiply By	100	Equals	Credit Utilization %
$3,000	÷	$10,000	X	100	=	30%

Here's how credit utilization affects your credit score:

- **High credit utilization can lower your score**. Credit scoring models see high credit utilization as a sign of higher financial risk. It suggests that you may be relying heavily on credit and might have difficulty managing debt.
- **Ideal credit utilization ratio.** Credit experts generally recommend keeping your credit utilization ratio below 30%. However, having a utilization rate way below this level shows lenders that you are managing credit responsibly.
- **Individual and overall utilization matters.** High utilization on a single credit card can be just as damaging as high overall utilization across multiple cards.
- **Lower your utilization.** Lowering your credit utilization by paying down credit card balances can improve your credit score over time. As you reduce your credit card debt, your utilization rate decreases.

Maintain a low credit utilization by keeping credit balances as low as possible in proportion to your credit limits.

Try it on your own: Let's calculate your credit utilization.

First, gather your credit statements or use your credit report. List your credit cards and lines of credit. Then add your credit balances together and do the same for the credit limits. Use the table shown here.

Combined Credit Balances	Divided By	Total Credit Limit	Multiply By	100	Equals	Credit Utilization %
$	÷	$	x	100	=	

Now that you better understand credit reports and scores, it's time to keep track of changes as they happen.

STEP 6: MONITORING YOUR CREDIT

Use a credit monitoring service to monitor your credit report and track your credit score effortlessly. These services offer a variety of tools and features to help you keep a watchful eye on your credit profiles. They consistently monitor one or all three of your credit reports, detecting potential fraudulent or unauthorized activities and alerting you of any changes that might impact your creditworthiness.

Some services go beyond the basics, providing additional perks like ID theft protection, insurance, monitoring for your Social Security number on the dark web, assistance in resolving fraud, and access to credit education resources.

You've got choices between free and paid options. I have my favorites. For a current list of the best credit monitoring services, visit thesmilemoney.com/book.

What to do next: Set up alerts and notifications once you've settled on a credit report monitoring service. It's essential to review these alerts promptly to catch issues early. Additionally, make it a habit to log on regularly (once a month will suffice) to stay on top of your credit status.

TAKE ACTION

1. Get one (1) free credit report from AnnualCreditReport.com.
2. Complete the Credit Report Review Checklist in the Appendix.
3. Get your credit score using a free credit monitoring app. For options, visit thesmilemoney.com/book.

 Enhance Your Credit Report and Scores Recap

In this chapter, you learned the essential parts of credit reports and scores. To recap, a credit report contains personal information such as your name, address, list of employers, credit inquiries, and the history and status of your credit accounts. A credit score simply represents numerical values for information found in your credit report.

You can also think of credit reports and scores in this way: a credit report is like the report cards you got at school that list the classes you've taken and how you're doing each semester. The credit score is your GPA, taking all that information and sharing it as a number, giving you an overall picture of how you're doing.

In this lesson you followed six steps:

- **Step 1:** Requesting your credit report
- **Step 2:** Reviewing your credit report
- **Step 3:** Disputing credit report inaccuracies
- **Step 4:** Getting your credit score
- **Step 5:** Improving your credit score
- **Step 6:** Monitoring your credit

You now have the knowledge to get your free credit reports and scores, dispute errors, and improve your credit health.

Congrats! You've just completed the lesson to enhance your credit report and scores. The next chapter will help you eliminate debt.

CHAPTER **12**

Eliminate Your Debt

redit offers choices. However, the uncontrollable use of other people's money can lead to overwhelming debt, resulting in fewer options. Debt takes up space in your mind and drains your energy. You want credit to push you forward, not hold you back.

Whether your debt is from a mortgage, student loans, or credit cards, studies show just the thought of debt can cause anxiety and psychological issues.[1] I've suffered with debt: it was debilitating. It makes it hard to think or do anything, let alone fix the situation. I used to only blame the creditors for my debt status because of their high interest rates and fees. And there were many creditors to place the blame on. Then I finally saw that the common denominator was me. I got myself into debt, and I was the key to getting myself out of it.

---

[1]"Financial Strain and Suicide Attempts in a Nationally Representative Sample of US Adults," *American Journal of Epidemiology* 189, no. 11 (November 2020), https://academic .oup.com/aje/article/189/11/1266/5874604

Now, the success of any debt payoff strategy starts with mindset—how you think and feel about money and your relationship to credit. You must identify the root cause of overspending, understand your reliance on credit cards, and recognize how that debt came to be.

In this chapter, you'll learn how to eliminate debt with the following steps:

- **Step 1:** Assessing your relationship to credit
- **Step 2:** Listing your debt obligations
- **Step 3:** Prioritizing your debt repayments
- **Step 4:** Paying off your credit cards
- **Step 5:** Freeing yourself from student loans
- **Step 6:** Owning your home free and clear
- **Step 7:** Breaking free from medical debt
- **Step 8:** Getting help with unmanageable debt

STEP 1: ASSESSING YOUR RELATIONSHIP TO CREDIT

Debt makes us feel all kinds of negative emotions. It can be embarrassing and is often associated with guilt. I want to relieve you of that shame. It may feel better to pretend everything is okay, but that will not give you the peace of mind you deserve.

How do you feel about your debt? Are you okay with it? Or do you feel overwhelmed? Anxious? Guilty? Or are you simply avoiding thinking about it in a way to suppress any negative feelings that may arise?

However you answered those questions or whatever thoughts came to mind, I want you to understand two things: acknowledge your role in getting into debt and accept your role in eliminating it. You see, the journey to debt freedom starts with changes to money beliefs and better financial habits. Because you are both the problem and the answer. It's up to you to act. And I am here to help guide you along the way. Before getting further into the steps, let's start with some fundamental money tips. These will support any debt-elimination strategy you choose.

▨ **Tip 1: Stop adding to your debt.**

Limit credit use, so you're not adding to your debt load. You can't eliminate debt if you're still adding to it. If you've done the cash flow calculation from the Manage Money pillar and learned that you're living above your means, you might be relying on credit cards to fill in the gap. Thus, cutting back on expenses is a must.

▨ **Tip 2: Reduce your expenses.**

Cut back on nonessential spending to positively affect your cash flow, and use the money towards debt repayment. The more money you can put towards debt, the faster you become debt-free. I did a spending freeze, which included cutting back all nonessentials for six months. I was able to use the unspent money to pay off the lower-balanced credit cards.

▨ **Tip 3: Increase your income.**

You can only cut expenses so much before it starts affecting you negatively. A big part of debt payoff success is motivation. So it's not good to deprive yourself of simple joys for too long. Instead, I want you to focus on increasing your income. Start by finding a side hustle. Go back to the Earn Money pillar for ideas.

▨ **Tip 4: Use found money.**

Put your bonus, commission, or unexpected cash (like the $20 you found in the pocket of that winter jacket) towards debt repayment. It might seem like a few dollars won't make a difference, but when it comes to debt elimination, every dollar does make a difference. In fact, it accelerates debt payoff.

STEP 2: LISTING YOUR DEBT OBLIGATIONS

You must identify and organize your existing debt. I've learned that many people often don't know the total debts they hold. This is a problem because you can't fix something you don't fully understand. I want you to list your debt expenses. You can refer to the expenses worksheet from the Manage Money pillar. If you haven't completed that exercise, use the table to list your existing debts or complete the worksheet found in the Appendix.

Expense List		
Outstanding Debt	**Monthly Expense Example**	**Your Monthly Expense**
Mortgage	$2,000	$
Car loan	$350	$
Student loan	$100	$
Personal loan	$100	$
Credit card	$75	$
Credit card	$35	$
Credit card	$25	$
Medical debt	$	$
Other:	$	$
Other:	$	$
Other:	$	$
Total	$2,685	$

STEP 3: PRIORITIZING YOUR DEBT REPAYMENTS

It's important to know that not all debts are created equal. Earlier in the pillar, you learned about the good, the bad, and the cred-ugly. Some debts will cost you more than others. So you should focus on paying off certain debts first. Use the following to determine the payoff priority and strategy to eliminate debt.

Debt Prioritization Strategy

While the repayment order will vary based on your personal circumstances, you can prioritize debt payoff in this way. Work on eliminating debts starting at number 1.

1. **Payday loans:** These often come with exorbitant interest rates. Eliminating payday loan debt should be a priority to avoid long-term financial strain.

2. **Credit card debt:** High-interest credit card balances can quickly spiral out of control. Paying off these debts early can prevent interest from piling up.

3. **Personal loans:** Depending on the interest rate, paying off personal loans early can free up money for other financial goals.

4. **Student loans:** While some student loans have manageable interest rates, focus on paying off higher-interest loans first.

5. **Mortgage and auto loans:** These loans typically have lower interest rates and longer repayment terms. While important, they can often be tackled after higher-interest debts are eliminated.

6. **Medical debt:** Pay these off according to interest rates and terms. Some have zero or low interest rates but have shorter terms. If the debt is in collections, a different strategy applies.

Debt Elimination Strategies

Whether you have credit card debt or installment loans, use the following debt elimination strategies:

- **Payoff high-interest debt first.** Start by tackling debts with the highest interest rates first, which is often credit cards. High-interest debt costs you more, so paying these off sooner saves you money.

- **Snowball and avalanche methods.** You can pay off smaller debts first regardless of interest or pay off debts with the highest interest first. Ultimately, it's about what method motivates you the most. You'll learn more about how to apply these methods to credit card debt in the following steps.

- **Consolidate balances.** Make credit card debt payments more manageable with a consolidation loan. Get the benefit of lower interest rates, better terms, and a lower monthly payment. Consolidation can positively impact your cash flow and lower the total cost of borrowing.

- **Refinance larger debts.** Refinance your debt into a lower-rate loan. Reduce your monthly payments and total cost of borrowing by refinancing your personal loans, auto loans, student loans, and mortgages.

■ **Negotiate with creditors.** Call your lenders and credit card issuers about lowering your current interest rates. Many have programs that help good customers with loyalty rate reductions, and others have options for borrowers who are facing financial distress.

■ **Appeal your medical bills.** Speak with your healthcare providers and insurance companies on how you can resolve your medical debt. There are options available to reduce or eliminate them.

I want you to know that you can use a combination of these strategies to eliminate debt sooner. For instance, you can negotiate with your credit card issuers for lower rates and apply the snowball or avalanche methods. This is the strategy I used to get rid of over a dozen credit card balances. I worked with my creditors to lower the interest rates, which lowered my monthly payment. It "freed" up money that helped me pay off the credit cards with the smallest balance first.

This is important for you to do: As you pay off your debts, it's crucial you celebrate each payoff milestone. Decide on how you'll celebrate, perhaps with a small treat. Remember, successful debt elimination requires motivation, consistency, and joy.

HOW TO PRIORITIZE YOUR DEBT REPAYMENTS

Here's a table showing how you can prioritize your debts. It's helpful to see debt based on balances and interest rates.

Debt Prioritization Worksheet				
Debt Type	Creditor	Outstanding Balance	Interest Rate	Minimum Monthly Payment
Mortgage	ABC Bank	$330,000	4%	$2,100
Car	Car Financing	$21,000	9%	$325
Credit card	US Credit	$5,000	19.99%	$165

Debt Prioritization Worksheet				
Debt Type	Creditor	Outstanding Balance	Interest Rate	Minimum Monthly Payment
Student loan	Federal	$10,000	6.25%	$95
Medical debt	State Hospital	$3,000	0%	$250
	Total	$369,000	Total	$2,685

Give it a try: Do the following.

- ▪ **List your debts:** Include credit card balances, loans, mortgages, medical bills, and any other outstanding obligations. Include the names of creditors, outstanding balances, interest rates, and minimum monthly payments.

- ▪ **Calculate total debt:** Add up the total amount you owe across all debts. This gives you a comprehensive view of your overall debt load.

Debt Prioritization Worksheet				
Debt Type	Creditor	Outstanding Balance	Interest Rate	Minimum Monthly Payment
		$		
		$		
		$		
		$		
	Total	$	Total	

You can also use the Debt Prioritization Worksheet found in the Appendix.

Let's now get into the specific strategies to get rid of the different types of debt you may have. In the following steps, you'll learn how to get rid of credit card balances and pay off student loans and mortgages, along with getting the support you may need for extreme unmanageable debt.

STEP 4: PAYING OFF YOUR CREDIT CARDS

Credit cards balances are often the hardest to eliminate. That's because of the open credit line and the higher interest rates associated with them. And here's the thing: if you only make the minimum monthly payments, a small balance carried month to month will balloon in size and cost you more. The good news is that there are strategies you can use to pay off your credit cards. And you'll learn them all starting with the simplest thing you can do.

Pay Extra Each Month

If you'd like to see how extra payments affect credit card balances, check out the Minimum Payment Warning in the Payment Information box printed on your credit card billing statement. By adding a few extra dollars to the minimum payment, you can pay off credit card debt in three years. In the example given, the estimated savings is $5,053.

Payment Information	
Payment Due Date Jan 11, 2024	For online and phone payments, the deadline is 8pm ET.
New Balance $3,410.61	Minimum Payment Due $114.00

LATE PAYMENT WARNING: If we do not receive your minimum payment by your due date, you may have to pay a late fee of up to $40.

MINIMUM PAYMENT WARNING
If you make only the minimum payment each period, you will pay more in interest and it will take longer to pay off your balance. For example:

If you make no additional charges using this card and each month you pay. . .	You will pay off the balance shown on this statement in about. . .	And you will end up paying an estimated total of. . .
Minimum Payment	18 Years	$10,014
$138	3 Years	$4,961
Estimated savings if balance is paid off in about 3 years: $5,053		

We often don't realize how an extra $10 or $20 towards repayment can make a big difference. It truly does. But where can you find extra dollars to add to your monthly payments? Cut back on some expenses (Manage Money pillar) or find a side hustle (Earn Money pillar).

Use Balance Transfers

Are you tired of managing multiple credit card balances, due dates, and interest rates? A balance transfer is a good strategy. You can take advantage of lower interest rates and consolidate multiple high-interest credit card balances onto a single card.

Many credit card companies offer promotional periods with significantly lower rates. Some even offer 0% interest rates on balance transfers. This means that for a specified period, you won't accrue interest on the transferred balance. But it depends on the card offer. Shop around for the best deal because rates vary and the interest-free period can range from months to a year or more.

This is how it works: With lower or no interest during the promotional period, more of your payments go towards reducing the principal (the actual debt amount) balance. It doesn't get eaten up by interest charges, which means you make quicker progress in paying down your debt.

Use a Debt Consolidation Loan

Instead of a balance transfer, another option is using a debt consolidation loan. It combines multiple high-interest credit card balances into a single loan with more favorable terms. The loan pays off your credit card debts in full. Some lenders might require closing the credit card accounts included in the consolidation. The purpose is to keep you from accumulating additional debt.

To get started, list all your credit card balances to determine how much you'll need to consolidate. Refer to the Appendix for a consolidation worksheet to help you. Afterwards, shop around for lenders. And compare interest rates, terms, and fees to find the best options. To find the right loan for you, visit phroogal.com.

Use the Debt Snowball Method

The debt snowball focuses on tackling the smallest balance first. After paying off the smallest balance, the monthly payment for that credit card is added to the repayment of the card with the next-smallest balance. This process continues until all cards are paid off.

Picture your payment to one card increasing each time you've paid off a balance. It's like a snowball growing larger as more snow is compacted. The snowball method is the one I used that helped me get rid of credit card debt. It's also the method that made the most sense to me. I needed to be motivated. And since I was able to celebrate paying off my first credit card quickly, it was motivating.

DEBT SNOWBALL EXAMPLE

Credit Card Name	Balance	Minimum Payment
Credit Card #1	$500	$25
Credit Card #2	$6,300	$146
Credit Card #3	$7,000	$200

How it works: After paying off Credit Card #1, you then apply the $25 minimum payment to Credit Card #2, making the total payment $171 ($146 + $25). Once you've paid off the second credit card balance, you add the $171 payment to the minimum monthly payment of Credit Card #3, totaling $371. By paying more than the minimum payment, you speed up balance payoff.

The debt snowball might not be the best choice mathematically because it doesn't pay attention to the interest rates. So it may cost you more to keep higher-rate credit card balances for longer as you pay off smaller-balance cards.

Use the Debt Avalanche Method

The debt avalanche method focuses on the repayment of debt with the highest interest first. You basically want to pay off the costliest balances. The method works like this: Once you've paid off the one with the highest interest, you move on to the second-highest-interest credit card. You continue to move down the list until all debts are paid off. Like the snowball method, you add all prior minimum payments from paid-off debt towards the following credit card balance, creating an avalanche of falling interest payments.

DEBT AVALANCHE EXAMPLE

Credit Card Name	Interest Rate	Balance	Minimum Payment
Credit Card #1	20.99%	$7,000	$200
Credit Card #2	14.99%	$6,300	$146
Credit Card #3	9.99%	$500	$25

How it works: After paying off Credit Card #1, you take the $200 minimum payment and apply it to Credit Card #2, making the total monthly payment $346 ($146 + $200). Once Credit Card #2 is paid off, you add that payment to Credit Card #3's minimum monthly payment ($200 + $146 + $25), totaling $371. Have more than three credit cards? Just continue the process.

I do want to note that the debt avalanche method makes the most mathematical sense. Because you're eliminating balances with the highest interest rate, it lowers the cost of the debt. However, math aside, motivations are quite different for each person. What will motivate you to get rid of your credit card balances?

Decide which credit card strategy works best for you. You can start with the snowball and switch to the avalanche method, or vice versa. I do recommend settling on one method sooner rather than later.

STEP 5: FREEING YOURSELF FROM STUDENT LOANS

Student loans are offered by federal and private lenders to help you pay for the cost of education. However, once the loan is funded, you work with student loan servicers—the companies responsible for managing and overseeing the repayment of student loans. Servicers are contracted by the federal government or private lenders who offered you the loans.

To begin this step, start by listing your student loans (or refer to your debt prioritization worksheet). You can access your federal student loan information through the US Department of Education website by visiting https://nsldsfap.ed.gov. For private student loans, review your credit report. Then use the following strategies.

Set Monthly Payment Reminders

Set up automatic bill payments for each month. Doing so avoids late fees and additional interest accruals that add to the total cost of borrowing. It ensures your student loan debt doesn't get more expensive.

With automatic payments, you won't miss a due date too. One missed payment can impact your credit score substantially. And a series of missed payments on federal loans can lead to default. Student loan default occurs after a period of nonpayment, typically 270 days (about 9 months). It can lead to legal actions, credit damage, and wage garnishment.

If you're having hardships or income disruptions, reach out to your loan servicers to learn about your options. Federal loans qualify for deferments, forbearance, and income-driven repayment plans. And some private loans may offer payment pause benefits or deferments as well.

Consolidate Federal Loans

If you have multiple loans or are paying more than one loan servicer, consolidation is a good strategy. Loan consolidation is a federal program that combines all your federal loans while keeping the benefits of income-driven repayment options, financial hardship programs, and loan forgiveness.

Consolidating federal loans is different than refinancing student loans. You may lose some federal repayment benefits if you decide to refinance federal and private loans together. Choose to consolidate federal loans and refinance private loans separately.

Refinance Student Loans

When you refinance student loans, you take out a completely new loan with a private lender. The monthly payment and cost of borrowing might decrease if you refinance at a lower interest rate and a shorter term. There are many private lenders offering student loan refinancing.

Throw in a Little Extra to Your Student Loans

With your existing student loans, add a few extra dollars with each minimum payment to lower the principal balance. And if you consolidated or refinanced your loans, you can also add extra to the new monthly payment. Essentially, you're combining payoff strategies to pay off student debts faster.

ENSURE YOUR EXTRA PAYMENTS ARE APPLIED CORRECTLY

Follow these steps:

1. Make the regular monthly payment by the due date to avoid late fees.
2. Make the extra payment on the same day as your regular monthly payment. Your regular payment will satisfy the accrued and unpaid interest, while your extra payment is applied directly to the principal balance.
3. Indicate the extra payment is towards the principal balance, not an early payment of next month's bill.
4. After the servicer processes the payment, review your account to ensure it was done correctly.

For example, you made a $200 standard repayment with a $50 extra payment. It's applied as:

- $190 repayment to accrued interest
- $10 repayment to the principal balance
- $50 extra payment to the principal balance

(Continued)

(*Continued*)

If fees apply to your situation, they will be paid first before standard repayments are applied to the principal balance.

- $190 repayment to accrued interest
- $5 applied to fees
- $5 repayment to the principal balance
- $50 extra payment to the principal balance

Paying extra may also reduce the Current Amount Due shown on your next billing statement(s). Even if there's no required amount due on the billing statement, continue to make payments to accelerate the payoff.

Applying for Student Loan Forgiveness

A program offered by the US government allows eligible borrowers to have a portion or the entirety of their federal student loans forgiven. It means they are no longer required to repay the remaining loan balance. Student loan forgiveness requires meeting specific criteria, such as working in certain public service professions, teaching in low-income schools, or making a specified number of qualifying payments under income-driven repayment plans. For more details on this program, I recommend visiting studentaid.gov.

HOW TO MANAGE YOUR FEDERAL STUDENT LOAN PAYMENTS

If you find it difficult to pay your monthly payments for federal student loans, you can sign up for an income-driven repayment plan. The plans adjust your monthly payment to a manageable level according to your income and the size of your family.

Each plan has an eligibility requirement you must meet to qualify. The four income-driven repayment plans are:

Saving on a Valuable Education (SAVE) Plan: Any borrower with eligible federal student loans can enroll. The monthly payment is generally a percentage of your discretionary income. It's the most generous repayment plan offered.

Income-Contingent Repayment (ICR) Plan: Any borrower with eligible federal student loans can make payments under this plan. The monthly payment will be the lesser of 20% of your discretionary income or what you would pay on a repayment plan with a fixed payment over 12 years, adjusted according to your income.

Pay as You Earn (PAYE) Repayment Plan: The monthly payment is generally 10% of your discretionary income but never more than the 10-year Standard Repayment Plan amount.

Income-Based Repayment (IBR) Plan: Monthly payment is generally 10–15% of your discretionary income depending on whether you're a new or existing borrower on or after July 1, 2014. It's never more than the 10-year Standard Repayment Plan amount.

In any income-driven repayment plan, your monthly payment might go up or down if your income or family size changes annually. You need to "recertify" your income and family size every year.

Student loan forgiveness

Under all four plans, any remaining loan balance is forgiven if they aren't fully repaid at the end of the repayment period. Repayment requirements vary.

The federal student aid website (studentaid.gov) and your loan servicer can provide more detailed information. They can help you choose the right income-driven repayment option and review qualifications for loan forgiveness.

STEP 6: OWNING YOUR HOME FREE AND CLEAR

Home loans, such as mortgages and home equity loans, are low priority in debt repayment because of lower interest rates and potential tax benefits. However, the prospect of owning your home outright is an exciting goal. Some strategies to achieve a mortgage-free life include the following.

Make Extra Payments

One of the most straightforward methods to pay off your mortgage faster is by making extra payments. You'll pay less interest over the life of the loan and may have the house mortgage-free years before the original term. Even small additional amounts can make a significant impact over time. Consider these approaches:

- **Biweekly payments:** Split your monthly mortgage payment in half and pay that amount every two weeks. This results in 26 half-payments (equivalent to 13 full payments) per year, helping you make an extra payment annually.
- **Round-up payments:** Round up your monthly payment to the nearest hundred or even the nearest fifty dollars. The extra amount can go directly towards reducing your principal balance.

Make Principal-Only Payments

Some lenders allow you to make additional payments that go towards the principal balance, separate from your regular monthly payments. This strategy directly reduces your loan balance and changes the mortgage amortization schedule, leading to a faster payoff.

- Each time you get extra income or unexpected funds from bonuses, tax refunds, and found money, pay it directly to your principal balance.

Refinance to a Shorter Term

Refinancing your mortgage to a shorter loan term, such as a 15-year instead of a 30-year mortgage, can help you pay off loans faster. While monthly payments might be higher, you'll likely benefit from a lower interest rate and save a substantial amount on interest over the life of the loan.

HOUSE HACKING TO MORTGAGE FREEDOM

House hacking is a real estate investment strategy where you live in the house and rent out rooms that cover the total cost of your mortgage. Essentially, your roommates pay for the mortgage, allowing you to use your income differently. Use the following tips:

- **Vet your renters carefully.** You want responsible people who will pay their bills and won't require much effort to collect rent.
- **Draft an agreement.** Set the payment amounts, terms, and rules of living in the house. Get familiar with local laws and ordinances.
- **Require rental insurance.** Your homeowner's insurance may not cover your renter's belongings in case of disaster.
- **Budget for repairs.** You'll need money to fix issues around the house because of the wear and tear caused by multiple people living there.

STEP 7: BREAK FREE FROM MEDICAL DEBT

A few years ago, my parents had medical emergencies that landed them in the hospital, and then a series of doctor visits and a life-changing diagnosis led to a mountain of medical debt. I remember my parents saying the diagnosis came as a surprise, but the medical bills were an even bigger shock. The debt spiraled out of control, and the constant collection calls became harmful. After speaking with an attorney, we realized the best approach was to file for bankruptcy to alleviate the financial stress so they could focus on their health.

My parents aren't alone. The Consumer Financial Protection Bureau states that one in five households have overdue medical debt. It is one of the greatest stressors faced by millions of people.

While having medical debt is overwhelming, there are things you can do to protect yourself and ways to get rid of medical debt once and for all.

First, you want to review your medical bills carefully. Mistakes do happen and there's a good chance you're being billed incorrectly. You could be billed for a different health condition or be billed for a treatment you didn't receive. Always request an itemized copy of your bill and scrutinize it for accuracy. And verify that your name, insurance information, and billing address are correct.

Second, negotiate with the providers. Many healthcare providers are willing to set up a payment plan or offer a discount. Speak with someone in the billing department to discuss your options.

Third, ask about financial assistance or hardship programs. Hospitals and healthcare providers may offer charity care based on need and income level. The program can significantly lower the cost or eliminate the medical bill if the patient cannot afford it. In fact, nonprofit hospitals are required by law to provide some kind of financial assistance.

Finally, work with a medical bill advocate. They are experts who know the medical billing world, can review your statements, and negotiate for you. This is best for those who have thousands of dollars in medical debt. Be wary of scammers, though, so do your homework to find the right advocate.

 Your Medical Debt and Collection Agencies

If your medical debt is with a collection's agency, you have options:

- Request a verification of the medical debt. Mistakes are common, so make sure it really does belong to you.
- Dispute amounts that make no sense. Contact your healthcare providers for itemized bills and your insurance company for assistance.
- Negotiate with the collection agency on a drastically reduced bill if paid in full or a payment plan that works for you.
- Seek legal assistance to protect yourself before the collectors file a lawsuit against you.

It's important to know the following:

- Collection agencies can contact you to collect the debt but cannot threaten or harass you. If you're being harassed, contact the Consumer Financial Protection Bureau (consumerfinance.gov).

- Don't agree to any terms you cannot afford. Be realistic with yourself and firm with the collectors.
- Due to recent changes in federal law, medical debt no longer appears in your credit report and is not factored into your credit score.

STEP 8: GETTING HELP WITH UNMANAGEABLE DEBT

If the thought of debt keeps you up at night, I want you to know there is an answer to your debt situation. As my friend Melanie Lockert, author of *Dear Debt*, has said, "You are not a loan. You are not alone." Help is available and offered by many professionals.

You can get support from credit counselors, money coaches, and financial therapists. These experts help you understand your thoughts, teach you stress-coping techniques, provide guidance, and share solutions. Additionally, there are debt management plans offered by nonprofit credit counseling organizations. You can also speak with an attorney to learn about bankruptcy protection.

Knowing what resources are available can help you move forward and regain control over your finances. I want you to consider the following options.

Work with a Debt Coach or Counselor

Debt coaches or counselors develop strategies to address your debt, improve your financial habits, and work with you to achieve your goals. They go beyond simply giving advice and offer actionable personalized steps.

Use a Debt Management Plan

A debt management plan (DMP) is a structured program offered by credit counseling agencies to help individuals struggling with unmanageable debts. With a DMP, the agency negotiates with creditors to get them to lower interest rates, remove fees, and create a consolidated repayment plan. DMPs usually last from three to five years. Under a DMP, you're required to make a payment to the agency each month which repays your debts according to a repayment plan made with your creditors.

Speak with a Bankruptcy Attorney

If your debt is overwhelmingly impacting your health, speak with a bankruptcy attorney. Learn about your rights under the law and options available. Bankruptcy is a big decision. There are consequences to filing, but the benefits of doing so may outweigh them. As with any area of the law, it is crucial to select an experienced attorney to respond to your situation. Don't be ashamed to admit you've created insurmountable debt and need help. Ultimately, bankruptcy is about income reallocation and asset protection.

With that in mind, bankruptcy does come with a lot of social stigmas. There is shame, guilt, and embarrassment attached to it. But don't let the fear of judgment, comments from others, or people without knowledge of your situation deter you from using your legal rights and doing what's best for you.

TAKE ACTION

1. Complete the Debt Prioritization Worksheet found in the Appendix.
2. Use the methods you've learned to begin repaying your debt strategically.

 Eliminate Your Debt Recap

Debt can hold you back from doing more of the things that make you smile. It's a burden you might be carrying for far longer than necessary. In this chapter, you learned the steps to eliminate debt and free yourself of that burden.

I began the lesson to shift your mindset, challenging you to think like a wealth creator, not a debt accumulator, and continued with step-by-step guidance to get rid of debt:

- **Step 1:** Assessing your relationship to credit
- **Step 2:** Listing your debt obligations
- **Step 3:** Prioritizing your debt repayments
- **Step 4:** Paying off your credit cards
- **Step 5:** Freeing yourself from student loans
- **Step 6:** Owning your home free and clear
- **Step 7:** Break free from medical debt
- **Step 8:** Getting help with unmanageable debt

When it comes to getting rid of debt, it's vital to know your options and the resources available. It's equally important to think optimistically. Debt elimination doesn't happen in a day. It takes time, consistency, and persistence. Stay positive and believe you can do what some believe is impossible.

BORROW MONEY SUMMARY

Congrats on completing the lessons! You gained a great deal of knowledge to borrow better, improve credit, and lower stress associated with debt. Mastering the credit tool and not having it control you is how you make your money smile.

In the Borrow Money pillar, you learned credit can be a wealth creation tool. By using debt as leverage, you can purchase appreciating or income-producing assets. You also gained a better understanding of financing options, how credit reports and scores work, and strategies to eliminate debt. To recap, the pillar presented these lessons:

- **Lesson 1:** Use Your Leverage
- **Lesson 2:** Enhance Your Credit Report and Credit Score
- **Lesson 3:** Eliminate Your Debt

I want to remind you of these things: You are more than your score. You are more than your debt. You are so much more. Understanding the role of credit and how to use it properly improves financial health. Continuing your path to reducing and eliminating debt strengthens your financial well-being.

In the next pillar, Protect Money, you'll learn how to safeguard your identity, insure your assets, and plan your legacy.

PILLAR **V**

Protect Money

*L*egacy Strategy

While most financial discussions center on ways to earn and grow money, we must not forget about protecting it.

I've met many people who've shared stories on topics from stolen identities to inheritance issues. You might have stories of your own. People don't really think about protecting what they have because there's a limiting belief that they don't have much to protect. Well, you'll come to learn you have many things worth protecting.

The fifth pillar is Protect Money—your legacy strategy.

Protect Money	*Securing your legacy, protecting your family, and supporting your peace of mind.*

As you build wealth, think about safeguarding your most important assets—like your identity, money, family, and what you leave behind for future generations. It's not just about making money; it's also about ensuring you keep what you've earned safe and secure.

In the Protect Money pillar, you'll learn these lessons:

- **Lesson 1:** Safeguard Your Identity
- **Lesson 2:** Insure Your Assets
- **Lesson 3:** Plan Your Legacy

Before diving into the lessons, let's define what assets are in the context of financial wealth. Assets are things you own of value. It basically means someone else is willing to pay a price for it. For instance, your house is an asset but your family photo album is not. We can argue that both have value. However, unless you're someone famous, there isn't someone else willing to exchange money for your album as they would for a house.

So what things must be protected? Well, it requires knowing your net worth—the true signifier of financial wealth. Your net worth is what's left over after subtracting your liabilities from your assets. A positive net worth means you're building wealth. You can calculate it using the following equation:

$$\text{Net Worth} = \text{Assets}(\text{What You Own}) - \text{Liabilities}(\text{What You Owe})$$

When calculating your net worth, you list your assets and liabilities. Doing so provides insight. Your list of assets is a compilation of valuable items—things worth protecting. Meanwhile, your list of liabilities underscores your financial responsibilities—things that must be repaid. The interplay between your assets and liabilities determines the appropriate insurance coverages. It also shapes your preferences after your death.

There's a lot we'll cover in this pillar, so let's get protecting!

CHAPTER **13**

Safeguard Your Identity

dentity theft is when your personal information is used to commit fraud, such as opening new credit accounts, applying for loans, and using your identity to receive benefits. It's the type of fraud that uses your name, Social Security number, or credit card information.

"Sorry, man, your card was declined," said the gas station attendant.

I was worried. I parked the car and immediately called my credit card company. That's when I learned my card was frozen for suspicious activity. Someone was attempting an account takeover. These scammers weren't simply trying to use my credit card but requested an address change, email, and phone update. I was almost a victim of identity theft.

Fortunately, there were safeguards in place with my credit card to protect me. The unfortunate reality is that identity thieves will continue to attempt to get personal data somehow. Thieves will hack companies, rummage through garbage, send fake emails, and make threatening phone calls. Sometimes it seems like a losing battle, but we shouldn't give up. We can take steps to make it harder for these thieves to steal our information. In this chapter, you'll learn three steps to protect and regain your identity:

- **Step 1:** Securing your personal information
- **Step 2:** Keeping your data safe from scammers
- **Step 3:** Regaining your identity after fraud

STEP 1: SECURING YOUR PERSONAL INFORMATION

Identity thieves continue to invent new ways to steal personal data. You must know the following tactics to protect yourself:

- Family members using your personal information to open accounts without your knowledge or consent
- Phishing, which is the attempt to get your personal or financial information by having you respond to internet pop-ups or email spam
- Stealing your wallet or purse
- Vishing, which is the attempt to get your personal and financial information using the telephone
- Direct messaging scams threatening to expose naked photos or information about you
- Stealing your mail that may include pre-approved credit card offers
- Completing a change of address form and collecting your mail
- Looking over your shoulder while you take money out of an ATM
- Creating fake websites requiring you to enter your personal information
- Setting up fake job offers that require you to complete an application used to steal your identity
- Creating fake apartment rental listings to get you to fill out an application or pay a fee

- Setting up Wi-Fi hot spots that allow thieves to peak into your connected mobile device
- Using credit card and debit card skimmers that copy the information found on your card's magnetic stripe

As you've read, there are many ways to steal your information. It's exhausting just thinking about it. The good news is that there are things you can do. Use the following checklist to secure your information.

✓	Securing Your Personal Information Checklist	
	Set up account alerts.	Many creditors, banks, and credit unions offer alerts to notify you of transactions, ranging from deposits to withdrawals to purchases and payments. You can quickly spot issues before they become major problems.
	Limit sharing your Social Security number.	Don't share your number with anyone who isn't authorized. Always ask why your Social Security number is required.
	Shred your statements.	Dispose of financial statements, credit card statements, pay stubs, and bank records properly. Black out any identifying information such as your name, address, and account numbers. If possible, shred the documents.
	Use credit cards for purchases.	With credit cards, you get more legal protection compared to debit cards. In the event of fraud, you're not out of money in your checking account. Many card companies offer zero liability and an easy dispute process.
	Enroll your numbers on the Do Not Call Registry. Visit donotcall.gov.	Limit the number of companies calling you. The National Do Not Call Registry is a government registry that allows you to enter your home and cell phone numbers to prevent telemarketing calls.
	Monitor your credit report regularly.	Consider using a credit monitoring service that tracks the information found in your report and sends alerts and notifications of changes. There are free and paid services available.
	Enroll in an identity theft protection service and insurance.	These paid services monitor your email and Social Security number on the dark web. They notify you when your personal info appears on these sites. They also provide fraud resolution support and insurance for covered losses.

STEP 2: KEEPING YOUR DATA SAFE FROM SCAMMERS

I kept having missed calls with no one leaving messages. One day I picked up a call, and a man said, "Hi, this is Visa Mastercard Bank. We're calling about your Visa MasterCard account."

Playing along, I asked, "What about my card?"

"We need to verify recent purchases," the man said, "We need to confirm your identity first. What is your Social Security number?"

I knew this was a scam. First and foremost, there is no Visa Mastercard Bank. So I took this opportunity to give the scammer a lesson on ethical living, which he didn't take too kindly. He yelled at me and hung up.

Scammers are using every tactic imaginable to confuse you into giving personal information. Scams continue to operate because they successfully con millions of dollars from people and businesses yearly. There are many different types of scams, some elaborate and others seemingly simple. Here are some tips to increase your awareness of scammer tactics:

- **Be socially aware.** Don't share too much personal information on social media, like the financial services you use, and don't post answers to questions that can be used to guess your password or the answers to your security questions.

- **Say no to direct messages.** Scammers use social media DMs to get you to reveal passwords to social and financial accounts. Some of these messages might come from a hacked friend's account asking you to share sensitive information. And some direct messages can also be threatening, such as saying they'll reveal naked photos unless you send money.

- **Don't fall prey to email scams.** From the "we need your help" messages to phishing attempts, these scams ask you to reply to them or click on a link that redirects you to sites stealing your logins and passwords.

- **Watch out for fake websites.** Never click on a link in an email or DM that sends you a login request. Always go directly to the website and verify the URL before trying to log in or use the app. Report the messages to your financial institution. It can help them identify potential threats and shut down fraudulent websites.

- **Mind the phone scams.** Don't share personal info with callers. Remember, they called you and should have all the information they need.

- **Save yourself from social scams.** Scammers use social media to get you to click on links that either download viruses or ask for your login and password. They may also pretend to be someone you know or an influencer you follow.

- **Scan the texts.** Don't respond to or click on links in text messages or direct messages from unknown numbers and people.

- **Don't share one-time verification codes.** Never provide the codes to anyone asking for them. These codes are sent to you as part of two-factor authentication. Revealing them to others is a significant risk.

- **Inheritance pending.** Delete the emails about an inheritance that requires personal information and access to your banking accounts.

- **Love can cost you.** Be wary of people romancing you online and asking you to deposit checks and wire money to them.

- **Investment opportunities.** Watch out for scammers promising big returns, profits, or easy money by investing with them or someone they recommend. Ignore and block.

The biggest scams involve fraudsters pretending to be US government officials. The IRS, the Social Security Administration, and other government agencies have stated they will never call, text, or email messages asking for payment or identity verification. You will not be threatened with arrest. It's also important to know the IRS does not initiate contact with taxpayers through email, telephone calls, text messages, or social media.

Complete this checklist to help keep your data safe.

✓	Keeping Your Data Safe Checklist	
	Review financial and billing statements.	Look closely for charges you did not make. Even a small charge can be a warning sign. Thieves sometimes will make a small debit against your checking account and charge more if the small amount goes unnoticed.
	Request credit reports.	Get a copy of your free credit reports from AnnualCredit-Report.com. Review the details (refer back to the Borrow Money pillar). Look for names, addresses, and accounts you don't recognize.
	Don't ignore bills from any creditors.	A mysterious billing statement may be an indication that someone else has opened an account in your name. Contact the creditor immediately.
	Protect your PINs and other passwords.	Avoid using easily available information such as your mother's maiden name, birth date, the last four digits of your Social Security number, and phone number. Identity thieves can use this information to access your accounts.
	Use multiple email accounts.	Use different emails for personal use, social media, financial accounts, and subscription services. You may also have separate emails for newsletters and marketing offers.
	Use different passwords.	Have different passwords to prevent scammers from hacking into other accounts. Using a password management service can be useful.
	Place a security freeze.	If you're not looking at applying or opening new credit accounts, consider placing a security freeze on your credit profiles. It prevents new creditors from accessing your credit file.
	Remove your name from marketing offers. Visit optout-prescreen.com	Opting out prevents consumer credit reporting agencies from providing your credit file information to marketers for prescreened offers.

STEP 3: REGAINING YOUR IDENTITY AFTER FRAUD

What happens if your information is used fraudulently? Take a few moments to collect yourself. It is an extremely stressful situation. Now, take a few slow, deep breaths. I want you to know that you have options to regain your identity.

Start by gathering any documents related to the theft. Have information related to dates, times, and people you've contacted for a proper timeline of events. Then follow these five steps:

First, Contact the Place Where the Fraud Occurred

Let them know someone has stolen your personal information, and request the accounts be closed or frozen so no new charges are made. Contacting the creditor might be enough to resolve fraud involving one credit card. However, if the fraud encompasses more than transactions on a credit card, continue to the next steps.

Second, Place a Fraud Alert on Your Credit Reports

Contact one of the credit bureaus and they'll inform the other two. You can place a free, one-year alert on your credit profile. A fraud alert requires businesses to verify your identity before opening a new account, issuing an additional card, or increasing the credit limit on an existing account. An alert makes it harder for someone to commit fraud.

Third, Order Your Credit Report

If you file a fraud alert, you're entitled to a free report from all three major credit bureaus.

Credit Bureau	Website	Telephone
Experian	www.experian.com	(888) 397-3742
TransUnion	www.transunion.com	(800) 916-8800
Equifax	www.equifax.com	(866) 349-5191

Fourth, Review Your Credit Report

Make notes on any activity that you do not recognize. If you discover additional possible fraudulent activity, contact the lender or organization directly. Reach out to their fraud department and follow up in writing.

Finally, Create an Identity Theft Report

You can go to the Federal Trade Commission (FTC) website at identitytheft.gov to report identity theft and get a recovery plan and affidavit. Print the affidavit and provide it to creditors, credit bureaus, or police. In some municipalities, you can report ID theft at the police station. Your affidavit and police report make up your identity theft report.

If you have identity theft protection (either paid or free), contact the service provider and let them know what has happened. These services offer fraud resolution support.

EXTENDED FRAUD ALERTS

You can get an extended fraud alert on your credit file if you've created an Identity Theft Report. When you place an extended alert, you can get two free credit reports within 12 months from each of the three credit bureaus. The bureaus must take your name off marketing lists for prescreened credit offers for five years unless you ask them to put your name back on the list. The extended alert lasts for seven years.

TAKE ACTION

1. Complete the Securing Your Personal Information Checklist.
2. Complete the Keeping Your Data Safe Checklist.
3. Visit thesmilemoney.com/book for updated resources mentioned in this lesson.

 ### Safeguard Your Identity Recap

In summary, identity theft is when your personal information is used to commit fraud, such as opening new credit accounts, applying for loans, and using your identity to receive benefits. There are things you can do to protect yourself and make it harder for identity thieves to steal and use your personal data. Through this lesson, you learned the following:

▪ **Step 1:** Securing your personal information

> ▪ **Step 2:** Keeping your data safe from scammers
> ▪ **Step 3:** Regaining your identity after fraud
>
> Stay vigilant because scammers will continue to use every tactic imaginable to steal your good name and do some financial harm.

You've done it! You completed the lesson to safeguard your identity. In the next chapter, you'll learn how to insure your most prized possessions, from physical stuff to loved ones.

CHAPTER **14**

Insure Your Assets

'll be upfront with you: insurance is something you pay for that you really don't want to use. Because when you do, it's often associated with an emergency or a disaster. Insurance is there for peace of mind when calamity hits. It's meant to take away the financial aspect of the situation so you can focus on rebuilding and healing.

How are you protecting yourself?

My best friend Leo has repeatedly shared how much he loves USAA. He's been insured with them since he joined the US Navy years ago. Being in the military, Leo has moved around quite a bit. During those moves, he experienced unfortunate events that would have caused significant financial stress. But because he had insurance, the impact of those emergencies was less severe.

One time, Leo's car was in a hit-and-run while parked in front of his military housing near the Great Lakes Naval Base. "I didn't have to worry," Leo said, "USAA took care of it right away." His car insurance covered a rental car. And when his car was broken into, his renter's insurance covered the stolen items, such as his laptop.

Then there was another time when Leo and I were in a flash flood during Hurricane Henri in New Jersey. We were submerged in under three feet of water. His car was considered a total wreck. He received an insurance payout that helped him buy a new car.

Insurance is really about mitigating risks. And it's secured by the payment of a regularly scheduled premium. Why have insurance? It's about protecting yourself against a specific loss, such as fire, wind, water, and so on over a period of time.

Which raises the question: how much insurance do you need?

"You don't need a lot of insurance," says Josh Bannerman, a CFP® professional and founder of Bannerman Wealth. "You just need the correct type and right amount of insurance to protect yourself from unforeseen hardships and losses."

I had the opportunity to speak with Josh, better known as "OG" on the Stacking Benjamins podcast, about protecting myself and my assets. Josh has over 25 years of financial planning experience. The conversation helped me understand insurance without feeling overwhelmed.

You know exactly what I mean: it's daunting to think about insurance because it sounds complex. Well, you're in luck, because this lesson will make it easy to grasp the essentials of insurance coverage.

To get started, I want you to know about the common types of insurance available.

Insurance Type	Description
Auto Insurance	Protects you in case of an accident, injuries to others, or damage to property in an auto accident. It can also protect your car if it is damaged or stolen.
Disability Insurance	Replaces a portion of income when you're unable to work because of illness or injury.
Health Insurance	Covers specific medical costs associated with illness, injury, and disability.
Homeowner's Insurance	Provides property damage and liability coverage under specific circumstances, including fire, storms, or other damages, with protection against negligence claims or inappropriate action.
Life Insurance	Protects dependents from loss of income, debt repayment, and other expenses after the death of the insured person. It includes term life or permanent life (e.g., 15-year and whole life policies).

Insurance Type	Description
Long-Term Care Insurance	Helps pay for expenses for in-home care, adult daycare, or nursing home residence.
Renter's Insurance	Protects from losses due to damage to the contents of a dwelling rather than to the dwelling itself.

In this chapter, you'll learn how to insure your possessions and protect your loved ones in 7 steps.

- **Step 1:** Protecting your money from inflation
- **Step 2:** Protecting your savings
- **Step 3:** Protecting your income
- **Step 4:** Protecting your stuff
- **Step 5:** Protecting your loved ones
- **Step 6:** Protecting your later years
- **Step 7:** Working with an insurance expert

STEP 1: PROTECTING YOUR MONEY FROM INFLATION

Inflation erodes the purchasing power of your money over time. Imagine if your favorite coffee used to cost $4 a cup, but now it costs $5 for the same treat. That's inflation at work. In simple terms, inflation is the gradual increase in the prices of goods and services. It's considered a normal part of a growing economy.

However, if the price of goods increases quickly, like if the cup of coffee went from $4 to $7, then we're in a high inflationary time. We've experienced this after the quarantine and shutdowns due to Covid. It means stuff has gotten more expensive. We're able to afford much less.

Whether normal or high, inflation does affect your financial well-being.

Firstly, it reduces the value of your savings. The interest you earn may not keep up with rising prices, causing your savings to lose value. Secondly, it can increase the cost of living. As prices go up, you might need to spend more on everyday things like groceries, gas, or rent, leaving less money for other things. Lastly, inflation can eat into your investments. Stocks, bonds, and other investments might not grow as fast as you hoped, meaning your money might not work as hard for you.

I don't want you to worry, though. There are things you can do to fight against inflation. You've learned many of these things throughout the Smile Money Pillars. Here's a recap of what you can do to protect your money from inflation:

- **Manage:** Keep a close eye on your spending and build a budget. Save and invest regularly, aiming to grow your wealth faster than inflation eats away at it.
- **Earn:** Increase your income and seek opportunities such as getting a better-paying job, starting a side hustle, or investing in your education and skills.
- **Grow:** Consider investing in assets like stocks, real estate, or bonds that historically have shown the ability to outpace inflation over the long term.
- **Borrow:** During high inflation, borrowing can offer potential benefits in terms of lower real interest rates and the opportunity to invest.

Again, inflation is a natural part of the economy. It's something we all have to deal with. Knowing how inflation affects your personal finances can help you protect your financial health.

STEP 2: PROTECTING YOUR SAVINGS

With bank failures in the news, it's vital to understand deposit insurance.

Is your money insured? The FDIC (banks) and NCUA (credit unions) offer insurance to participating financial institutions to protect your money from institutional failures. The FDIC and NCUA are independent federal agencies that govern and supervise financial institutions.

FDIC and NCUSIF (offered by NCUA) deposit insurance programs are quite similar. The standard insurance amount is $250,000 per depositor per insured financial institution, which means that if you have less than $250,000 in deposits at a single bank or credit union, your deposits are fully insured.

If you have over $250,000 deposited in one financial institution, you can do the following to ensure the FDIC or the NCUSIF covers your deposits.

- **Different ownership categories.** You can have accounts in different ownership categories to increase coverage, such as individual, joint, retirement, and trust accounts. For example, if you have a joint account with your spouse, the account would be insured up to $500,000 ($250,000 for your share and $250,000 for your spouse's share).
- **Multiple financial institutions.** Each participating financial institution is insured separately. You can spread your deposits to increase coverage. For example, if you have $500,000 in savings, you could open accounts at two different credit unions and deposit $250,000 in each account. This would ensure all your deposits are fully insured.

You don't have to "get" insurance to protect your savings. You must choose and deposit your money into an insured bank or credit union. To determine if your deposits are covered, speak with someone at your financial institution. Ask them to verify whether your deposits are fully insured. And inquire about what needs to be done if they aren't. Use the table shown here.

Financial Institution	Contact	Verified Coverage	Comments
ABC Bank *(example)*	800-123-4567	Yes, fully insured	

STEP 3: PROTECTING YOUR INCOME

Imagine if you suddenly fall ill or get injured, preventing you from working. Could you pay your bills? Without savings or any income coming in, you'll be stressing about two things: your health and your finances. That's when disability insurances comes into play. Disability insurance offers a bit of financial security by covering a portion of lost income. And depending on your coverage, it can support you for a span of months or even years.

Many employers offer disability insurance as a benefit but it can also be purchased individually through an insurance company.

I want you to do the following. Speak with your HR manager to learn about your disability insurance benefit. You can also consider getting individual disability insurance plans offered by insurance companies. Use this table and check the boxes once completed.

Disability Insurance Checkup		✓
Company	Verified disability insurance benefits with HR. How much are you covered? _____	
Personal (optional)	Researched individual disability insurance plans.	

STEP 4: PROTECTING YOUR STUFF

Review your auto, homeowner's, and/or renter's insurance to verify how much of your personal stuff is covered. Determine if your assets are covered in the event of damage or loss. Use the table provided.

Insurance Type	Insurance Company	Coverage Amount
Auto (example)	Gecko	Comprehensive coverage up to the market value of the car for total loss.
Home		
Auto		
Renter's		
Other:		

What else can you do? Make a list of all your items and their value. Store the list using a cloud drive service. I also recommend taking photos of your valuables and any related receipts. Upload them into the cloud too. Having this information will help you when filing a claim.

STEP 5: PROTECTING YOUR LOVED ONES

Do you have a life insurance policy? If you're a parent or have others who depend on you for financial support, having a policy will give you peace of mind knowing they'll be taken care of. Think of life insurance as a crucial safety net protecting your family's financial well-being. It ensures that your loved ones can feel financially secure when you're gone. Life insurance isn't for you, it's for them.

The amount of life insurance you need depends on your situation. While some people will boast they have a million-dollar policy, having that much insurance might not be right for you. But if you have a big family, younger children, and other unique situations, a larger policy might be needed, because you want to protect your family's finances. Life insurance can help your loved ones pay off a mortgage or any remaining debts. It can also be used to pay for living expenses or college tuition.

What Are Your Life Insurance Options?

You've probably heard about term life and permanent life insurance. The main difference between the two is how long they last. A **term life policy** covers you for a specific period, like 10 or 20 years, and pays out if you die during that time. A **permanent life insurance policy** lasts your whole life and has a cash value component that grows over time.

Choosing between the two depends on your needs. If you want coverage for a certain period, like until your kids are grown, term life might be better. A permanent life policy could be a better option if you want lifelong coverage and a savings component. Your decision should match your financial goals, budget, and how long you need the coverage.

It's also important to note that many life insurance companies offer variations of these policies. They may also refer to them using slightly different words. Knowing that there are two main types—term and permanent life insurance policies—will help you when discussing your options.

How Much Insurance Do You Actually Need?

"The amount of life insurance you need depends on your circumstances," says Josh Bannerman, CFP®. He adds that it's important to factor in age, income, family size, current debts, and future financial obligations, like paying for college. Hearing the word "depends" from Josh was comforting because the answer to how much insurance you need does indeed depend on your personal situation.

There are many online life insurance websites where you can get a quote. But I do recommend speaking with an insurance professional to help you determine the right amount. Doing so will help you narrow down your options. You can find additional resources at thesmilemoney .com/book.

There are two additional things I want you to know: 1) If you're feeling pressured by insurance salespeople to buy a policy, simply walk away. Many earn solely from commissions, and might use high-pressure tactics to get you to sign. If you don't understand what you're getting yourself into, don't get into it. And if it truly sounds too good to be true, then you might not have been given the full terms and conditions. 2) Don't rely solely on the life insurance offered through your employer. Many do offer a group-term life insurance as part of an employee benefits package. The death benefit to beneficiaries is often a multiple of your annual salary. It remains in effect as long as you're employed by the company. And if you're not, then you have no coverage.

HOW TO DETERMINE YOUR LIFE INSURANCE AMOUNT

You don't need much. You just need the right amount based on your situation.

1. **Assess your financial obligations.** Start by listing your financial responsibilities, such as outstanding debts (mortgage, loans), daily living expenses, education costs for children, and other ongoing financial commitments, and include funeral and burial costs.

2. **Calculate your income replacement.** Calculate how much of your income is needed by your family if you are no longer there to provide for them. A common guideline is to aim for 5 to 10 times your annual salary.

3. Account for future goals. Consider significant life events you want to support even after you're gone. These could include funding your children's higher education, affording a home, or ensuring your spouse's retirement.

STEP 6: PROTECTING YOUR LATER YEARS

Can you think about your life 30 or 40 years from now? It's a stretch for many, but doing that mental exercise is crucial.

Consider long-term care insurance to help you in your later years. It's a type of coverage designed to help cover the costs associated with extended care services, including assistance with daily activities like bathing, dressing, eating, or medical care due to chronic illnesses, disabilities, or cognitive impairments. Long-term care can be provided at home, or in assisted living facilities, nursing homes, or hospice care centers.

The cost of these services isn't typically covered by health insurance or Medicare. Without a policy, you could deplete your savings and burden your loved ones. Long-term care insurance can offer financial protection for you and your family.

HOW TO DETERMINE YOUR LONG-TERM CARE INSURANCE COVERAGE

1. **Consider your age.** Most financial experts start the conversation about LTC insurance at 50, but decisions about coverage may not happen until 60 years old.

2. **Assess your needs.** Evaluate your current health, family medical history, and potential long-term care needs. Consider factors like your age, overall health, and family support.

3. **Research providers.** Look for reputable insurers with positive customer reviews and a history of reliable service.

4. **Speak with a professional.** Talk to your advisor to guide you through the process and help you assess your needs.

STEP 7: WORKING WITH AN INSURANCE EXPERT

As you've read, there are different types of insurance, and you'll come across different insurance professionals. Some may offer car or home insurance, while others specifically focus on life insurance. Some work directly for insurance companies, while others work as your hired professional.

If you've scrolled through social media, you might have come across insurance salespeople using flashy videos and FOMO (fear of missing out) to get you to sign up for policies that seem beneficial to you. Be wary of them. I've seen some outright misrepresentations and bad advice.

So where can you get advice? There are insurance agents and insurance brokers. Both are licensed professionals and must abide by state laws and regulations. The key difference between brokers and agents is who they represent. Insurance brokers are independent professionals representing you, while insurance agents are employees of the company they represent.

Why Choose an Insurance Broker?

Insurance brokers will assess your risks and are legally obligated to help you select the best product. Brokers have the flexibility to offer a range of insurance options from many companies. They'll assess your needs, shop for the best policies, and advise you on the best fit. Brokers can earn a commission from the insurance company for each policy sold. Alternatively, you can use an online insurance broker. But as your needs evolve, it is helpful to work with a professional.

HOW TO FIND AN INSURANCE BROKER

A good place to start is to ask your family, friends, and colleagues for a referral. When working with an insurance broker, do the following:

1. **Know their fees.** Are they working based on commission only, or do they charge a service fee? Don't be afraid to ask this question early in the conversation.

2. **Verify their background.** Visit your state's Department of Insurance or Financial Services website to verify their state license. It's vital to do your due diligence.

3. Review complaints. Visit the state agency website and the Better Business Bureau for company reviews. Finding lots of unresolved complaints is a red flag on the type of service you'll receive.

If you're working with a financial planner, ask for an introduction to insurance experts, and do follow the same steps above.

TAKE ACTION

Use the worksheets in the Appendix to complete the action items.

1. Verify your existing insurance coverages.
2. Complete the insurance checklist.

 Insure Your Assets Recap

Insurance is meant to protect your peace of mind and financial security. It is a safety net for disaster and adversity, helping you and your loved ones cover financial obligations.

In this lesson, you learned that there are many different types of insurance products available, from protecting your deposits to supporting loved ones after your death. You also gained knowledge to protect your money, stuff, home, and family, through these steps:

- **Step 1:** Protecting your money from inflation
- **Step 2:** Protecting your savings
- **Step 3:** Protecting your income
- **Step 4:** Protecting your stuff
- **Step 5:** Protecting your loved ones
- **Step 6:** Protecting your later years
- **Step 7:** Working with an insurance expert

Remember, insurance is something you need and pay for, hoping never to have to use it. Because when you do, it's usually due to adversity. But having insurance is something you will be glad to have when the situation arises.

Congrats on completing the insurance lesson! In the next chapter, you'll learn to plan your legacy around taxes, estate planning, and how to create your money team.

CHAPTER **15**

Plan Your Legacy

t's said there are two things we can't avoid: death and taxes. And it's widely shared that there are two things we avoid talking about: money and death. I'm about to break both of these taboos at the same time.

Years ago, I was hospitalized while traveling for work. The nurse attending to me asked about a healthcare directive. I told her I didn't have one. She replied, "It's very important."

I didn't think much of it at the time. I was only concerned about getting better. But the look on her face and the words she emphasized ("It's. Very. Important.") stuck with me. So much so that when I got better, I wanted to understand why.

I've spoken to dozens of experts and heard many compelling stories from people all across the country. Some of their experiences were uplifting while others were heart-wrenching. All these conversations emphasized the importance of having legal documents outlining our wishes from when we're sick to when we die and beyond.

Speaking with estate planning experts led to learning about the tax liabilities of my wealth after dying. That led to deeper discussions with tax experts for a better overall tax strategy while I'm still alive. Now,

I understand the importance of both having a plan and a strategy for peace of mind. I can continue to grow wealth, minimize tax liabilities, and ensure my loved ones inherit the wealth I've created and carry out my wishes. And the good news is that you can do this too! In this chapter, I'll show you how through the following:

- **Step 1:** Creating your tax strategy
- **Step 2:** Building your estate plan
- **Step 3:** Choosing your money team

STEP 1: CREATING YOUR TAX STRATEGY

You won't escape taxes, but you can plan to minimize your tax liabilities.

When most people think of taxes, they're thinking about filing tax returns. But there's more to taxes than just filing and hoping for a refund. There is strategy involved to help you follow the tax code to keep more of your earnings and protect your wealth.

I spoke to Michael Jones, a Georgia-based certified public accountant and founder of Booked CPA & Co. He was referred to me by a friend and colleague, Crystal Orr, who is currently the president and CEO of the Urban League of Union County in New Jersey, where I also serve as a board member.

Michael explained that "a tax strategy is a tax-focused financial plan that helps you to forecast your taxable income, your tax owed, and ultimately your tax liability or tax refund, among other tax matters." It truly is about protecting what you've worked hard to make.

"There are tons of strategies and most require proper planning and implementation," Michael added. I've also learned that tax planning isn't something you start when you're filing returns early in the year. It's something you work on throughout the year with your accountant.

It can be daunting to think about taxes, but you don't have to do it alone. Whereas most financial plans focus on wealth building, a tax professional will zero in on the tax implications of the wealth you're creating. Speaking with a tax professional is best because tax rules can be complicated. And working with an accountant who understands the tax code, in Michael's words, "could literally transform just about anyone's financial outlook."

Now, it's possible you're not quite ready to sit down with a tax professional. But it's vital you understand how taxes affect your financial health. To get you started, the following are basic areas of taxes to know.

Improve Your Withholding

Our first relationship with taxes is through our paycheck, but we often don't adjust the withholding after the first day of the job. You can adjust your W-4 withholding at any time. So do it accordingly. If you have a huge tax bill after filing, you should *increase* your withholding. This can help you owe less in the next return. Alternatively, you could *reduce* your withholding if you had a big refund.

To update your withholding, you must contact your HR manager. Understand that they can't tell you how much to withhold or give you any tax advice. Alternatively, the IRS website has a tax withholding estimator. Try it out and see how your withholding amount affects your refund, take-home pay, or tax due. Go to irs.gov or thesmilemoney .com/book.

Retirement Planning Is Tax Planning

"The tax code is generally designed to stimulate the economy through government and state incentives," said Michael. "Take advantage of areas of the economy they have subsidized."

You can use tax-advantaged accounts to help you lower taxes today or minimize tax liability in retirement. I've covered these accounts in its entirety in the Grow Money pillar (go back to review, if needed). Here are two considerations:

- **Contribute to a 401(k) plan.** Most employers offer a retirement savings plan to help you invest towards retirement. Money is taken from your paycheck based on the percentage you've chosen. The plans are often pre-taxed, meaning your contributions lower your taxable income. Some employers offer to match some or all of your contributions. Think of it as additional money for your work.

▪ **Invest using an IRA.** You can access two additional retirement accounts outside of an employer-sponsored plan: traditional and Roth IRAs. With traditional IRAs, your contributions can be tax-deductible during the tax year it's filed. In contrast, Roth IRA contributions grow tax-free for withdrawal in retirement.

Now, regarding 401(k)s and IRAs, Michael emphasized it's important to "consider whether your contributions will fare better in one versus the other."

If you're wondering where to start, Michael shared a practical starting point: do an inventory of deductions, credits, and adjustments and determine which apply to you.

REDUCING YOUR TAXABLE INCOME WITH DEDUCTIONS

A tax deduction is an amount you can subtract from your taxable income, reducing how much tax you owe. It includes the following:

▪ **Retirement contributions.** If you contribute to a traditional IRA, your contributions may be tax-deductible. This means you can deduct the amount when filing taxes.

▪ **Health savings account (HSA) contributions.** If you have a high-deductible health plan (HDHP), you may be eligible to contribute to an HSA. Your contributions to an HSA, outside of an employer plan, are tax-deductible, which can help reduce your taxable income.

▪ **State and local taxes.** You can deduct state and local income, sales, and property taxes on your federal tax return, which can help reduce your taxable income.

▪ **Mortgage interest.** If you own a home and have a mortgage, you can deduct the interest you pay on your mortgage on your federal tax return.

▪ **Charitable donations.** If you donate money or property to a qualified charity, you can deduct the value of your donation on your federal tax return.

▪ **Student loan interest.** If you are paying off student loans, you may be able to deduct the loan interest you pay on your federal tax return.

■ **Business expenses.** If you are self-employed or have a side business, you can deduct business expenses such as office supplies, travel expenses, and equipment on your tax return.

As you've read, there is a lot of "if you" on the list because the answer to your tax situation will depend. And remember, tax laws can be complex and subject to change, so it's a good idea to consult a tax professional to ensure you take advantage of all available deductions.

Your tax strategy should evolve over time as your life situation changes. It should also adjust in line with tax laws, ensuring that you are continually paying the least amount of tax allowable.

Do You Need an Accountant?

It depends on your situation. For many, using a tax preparation software might be sufficient, but as your financial situation evolves, sit down with an expert to plan your strategy. An accountant provides a range of financial services specifically focused on reducing tax liabilities. Many have the experience to offer advice from business formation to retirement plans to investment strategies.

Now, working with an accountant depends on the complexity of your finances and largely on your income bracket. But if you got a promotion, bought a house, started a business, got married, or had children, working with a tax professional can be beneficial. Have a conversation with one and decide whether or not it's necessary right now.

You have options to work with an accountant or a certified public accountant (CPA). CPAs pass a rigorous CPA exam. CPAs are accountants, but not all accountants are CPAs. CPAs help people and businesses reach goals and act as auditors, business advisors, and tax and accounting consultants.

HOW TO FIND AN ACCOUNTANT

Start by asking your network. Ask your family, friends, and colleagues if they work with a certified public accountant. And if you're already working with a financial planner, ask for a referral.

There are four areas to consider:

1. **The first area is the specialty.** Find a CPA who works in your industry or niche. For example, if you have an e-commerce store, you'll want a CPA who understands the income and expenses of online businesses.
2. **The second area is identification status.** CPAs are given Preparer Tax Identification Numbers. The PTINs can be verified at IRS.gov to ensure your accountant is appropriately registered.
3. **The third area is services.** Accountants don't offer the same services. Ask what services are offered and determine if they match your needs. Are you looking for more guidance throughout the year, or are you solely focused on reducing taxes?
4. **The fourth consideration is the fees.** CPAs can charge a flat fee for filing taxes and may have a retainer or hourly rate for tax planning and consultations. Inquire about the prices and if they match your needs.

If you have a financial planner, introduce your CPA to them. They can work in tandem to help you reach your goals.

STEP 2: BUILDING YOUR ESTATE PLAN

If you got sick or died, how would your family know about your wishes, insurance policies, and assets? What are your funeral arrangements? Who will inherit the wealth you've built? How do you want to be remembered?

These questions are important to answer because they're vital for financial planning. I know how difficult it is to think about dying or being sick. But if we want to ensure our legacy, we can't avoid talking about the inevitable.

Estate planning is how you protect your legacy.

I want to put all the legal jargon aside. In its simplest form, estate planning is the preparation for transferring your stuff to loved ones in case of death or illness. The process starts with identifying all your assets and determining who in your family, friends, or organization would receive them. It includes:

- Identifying your loved ones as agents, trustees, or beneficiaries
- Listing your valuable assets and online accounts
- Writing your will and testament
- Having a financial power of attorney, healthcare POA, and living will
- Establishing a trust
- Adding joint owners and beneficiaries to assets

I enlisted the help of two estate planning experts to ensure the information I've shared here can guide you properly.

"Think about it this way. If you don't have a plan for your estate, the government already has a plan for it." said Courtney Richardson, a friend and attorney behind the Ivy Investor, a financial education platform. She added that your state has default laws that kick in after death or physical incapacitation. Many of these laws will not manage your estate as you want it to. If you don't want this to happen, creating a plan to manage your estate on your terms is best.

Now, you might be wondering if estate planning is even necessary for your situation because you don't have enough assets. I want to challenge that belief.

Diane Vidal wrote in an email that "estate planning is essential— for everybody." Diane is a Florida-based attorney specializing in estate planning and probate. She also happens to be an old high school friend.

"For example, young parents need to nominate a guardian for minor children in the event of their death; blended families should consider a trust to ensure the estate benefits both sides of the family. Everyone has a need for proper estate planning," Diane added.

It made me think: we *all* have something to protect and wishes we want carried out. Why not have a plan that lessens the stress related to money and ensures our affairs are settled? You don't have to leave it to guesswork on what you want to happen. You can outline your desired outcome.

Courtney and Diane detailed the two stages of estate planning: during life and after death. They both explained that during your life, the most important documents are your Revocable Trust, Durable Power of Attorney, Healthcare Surrogate, and Living Will. After your death, your Last Will and Testament and Trust will be of paramount importance.

Let's go over the two stages.

1. During Life

In this stage, you'll need to make the following decisions:

- What are your wishes in case of a medical emergency? These instructions relate to your wish to be placed or kept on life support.
- What are your wishes in case of incapacitation? These are instructions for who will manage your financial affairs if you become ill, injured, or unable to manage your finances due to age.

STAGE ONE: DURING LIFE

This part of your estate plan assigns someone to fulfill your wishes if you become physically incapable. In this stage, you may need to prepare two documents.

1. Durable Power of Attorney (POA): This document will allow you to designate an agent if you cannot handle your financial or medical affairs.

A **financial power of attorney** assigns a person to manage financial affairs if you're incapacitated. Without this POA document, you would have no one to manage your finances, such as paying bills, filing taxes, accessing bank and investment accounts, and other financial matters. The designated person (referred to as an agent) in your durable power of attorney can act on your behalf in financial situations.

If giving someone full control over your finances troubles you, consider a limited power of attorney. This legal document gives specific power to complete certain financial tasks.

A **healthcare power of attorney** is a signed legal document for when you can't make your own medical decisions. It names a single person as your healthcare decision-maker to make medical decisions such as choosing a doctor, accessing medical records, and putting you on life support.

You can opt to choose two different people for your medical and financial POA.

2. Advance Healthcare Directive: Also known as a living will, this is a document that outlines your wishes regarding medical care if you can no longer communicate. It's a statement of your wishes about life support and any kind of medical intervention that you do or don't want.

An Advance Directive works with your Durable Power of Attorney for healthcare decisions, enabling your chosen person to execute the medical decisions you've already established for your care.

Important things to remember:

- The names of these documents may differ, based on the state in which you live.
- Be mindful of whom you give power of attorney over your medical and financial affairs.
- Ensure that your banks and doctors have copies of the documents on file after creating them.

2. After Death

To prepare for this stage, you'll need to make the following decisions:

- Who will care for your children? You can assign guardianship and provide instructions to care for your minor children.
- Who do you want to leave your assets to? Identify and instruct how your wealth is distributed to your beneficiaries.

These decisions should not be left to the laws of the state where you reside. Your estate plan outlines your wishes, giving you peace of mind that they will be carried out.

STAGE TWO: AFTER DEATH

The second stage of your estate plan helps avoid chaos and messiness by clearly outlining your wishes.

1. Last Will and Testament (Will): This legal document outlines your wishes upon passing. Your will decides who inherits your property if no joint ownership or beneficiaries are listed on the assets. It can also name the guardians for young children.

In most states, your will goes through probate to assess validity. If there is no will, your assets go through a probate process. In a no-will scenario, state law and probate court determine the distribution of your assets and guardianship of minors.

2. Trust: A trust is a legal arrangement where you place your money, property, or valuable stuff in the care of someone you trust, known as a trustee. Think of this trustee as a special helper who follows your rules even after you're no longer around. Trusts are handy because they ensure your things go where you want them to, whether or not you're still alive. They're especially useful if you have a lot of valuable stuff you want to protect and manage the way you want. Trusts can also be a great tool if you need to look after someone with special needs, like a family member who requires extra care.

The following are the two most common:

Revocable Living Trusts provide flexibility and control. With this trust, you can make changes or even revoke it entirely during your lifetime. You maintain control over the assets you place into the trust and can manage them as you see fit. One of the primary benefits of a revocable trust is that it helps your assets pass to your beneficiaries without going through the often time-consuming probate process. Additionally, it offers privacy since the details of your assets and beneficiaries remain confidential.

On the other hand, **Irrevocable Living Trusts** are more permanent in nature. Once established, making significant changes or revoking the trust can be challenging. This type of trust may provide asset protection benefits, shielding some of your assets from creditors and potentially reducing estate taxes. However, in exchange for these benefits, you must relinquish control over the assets you place in the trust. While this may seem like a drawback, it can be a strategic move for those looking to safeguard assets or achieve specific tax advantages.

There are many trust types. With the help of an estate planning professional, you can decide which is best.

Other Ways to Pass Your Assets to Loved Ones

During the conversation with Courtney, she said, "We should think about how to protect our assets and peace of mind while we're still alive." So think about how your accounts are legally owned and the beneficiaries you assign to them.

Joint Ownership

For married couples, the common practice is to create joint accounts. This way, if one spouse passes away, the surviving spouse or the joint account holder becomes the full owner. If you add other people like children or grandchildren as joint owners, it can help you bypass the state's distribution process after you're gone, saving time and money. However, it's important to be cautious. This could lead to gift taxes and control over your belongings while you're still alive.

Beneficiaries

Having designated beneficiaries for your assets can often bypass the probate process and might supersede the last will and testament. It makes the transfer to your loved ones smoother. This approach applies to various accounts such as retirement plans, life insurance policies, and even certain bank accounts. Remember to keep your beneficiary designations updated to reflect any changes in your wishes or life circumstances (marriage, children, divorce, death).

HOW TO ADD BENEFICIARIES

Reach out to your financial institutions or custodians. And ask them about setting up payable-on-death beneficiaries. Make sure you name a beneficiary and contingent beneficiary. This simple step ensures your assets go directly to the intended recipients without the need for court involvement.

(Continued)

(Continued)

1. **Payable on death bank accounts:** Add PODs for all your bank accounts, including savings, checking, certificates, money markets, or any other money accounts you have with a financial institution.

2. **Transfer on death investing accounts:** Add a TOD beneficiary for your stocks, bonds, and brokerage accounts.

3. **Retirement plans like 401(k)s and IRAs:** Complete a beneficiary designation form for these accounts. Review and change beneficiaries for any life events (like marriage, divorce, children, etc.).

4. **Life insurance:** Designate a beneficiary for your life insurance and remember to update if necessary for life changes.

5. **Annuities:** Have your loved ones receive your annuities by designating who will receive any money left after your death.

Keep a list of your beneficiaries and inform them.

Don't Forget Your Digital Assets

After death, online profiles can be turned into legacy social media accounts. These accounts serve as a digital remembrance of the person and can include platforms like Facebook, Instagram, LinkedIn, and more.

Part of your legacy is the digital footprint you've left behind. Ensuring your online presence is accounted for in your estate plan is essential for closure. You can do two things:

1. **Designate a digital executor in your will.** Give family members or close friends access to your account to make certain updates and modifications after you pass away.

2. **Assign a legacy contact for your social media profiles.** Platforms like Facebook offer the option to memorialize an account. You can assign your family or friend as your legacy contact easily in the settings.

It's also important to know that smartphone companies like Apple offer owners a Legacy Contact for their Apple ID. Adding Legacy

Contact is the easiest way to give people you trust access to the data stored on your Apple account after you pass away.

Share Your Plan with a Loved One

It's important to establish an organized system so your loved ones know where to find documents and how to access your accounts. Start by creating a comprehensive document or digital file that outlines important information such as passwords, account details, estate plans, and other relevant instructions. This document can be stored securely in a designated location, such as a safe deposit box, a trusted attorney's office, or a digital password manager.

Communicate the existence and location of this document to a trusted family member, friend, or designated executor. Remember, if no one knows about the documents, it's harder for your plan to be executed.

Do You Need an Estate Planning Attorney?

A clear benefit of preparing an estate plan is the peace of mind that your assets will go to the rightful heirs. It can answer any questions your loved ones may have about your wishes.

And you have options to create one, from online services that provide you simple steps to fill the necessary legal documents to hiring an estate planning attorney to guide you through the entire process.

The benefit of working with an estate planning attorney is getting your questions answered and helping you feel good about the plan you're creating. These professionals can structure your legal document based on your situation and specific state requirements. And they can update the estate plan as needed because it isn't a one-and-done plan. It's a living document that needs to be reviewed, revised, and amended as your situation changes, such as significant life events—marriage, divorce, births, or deaths.

To create an estate plan, you can work with an estate planning attorney or use a DIY service. These services are listed on thesmilemoney.com/book.

HOW TO CHOOSE AN ESTATE PLANNING ATTORNEY

When searching for an estate planning attorney, there are three considerations:

1. **Reputation.** Get referrals to find a reputable and skilled estate planning attorney. Find three experts and schedule a time to interview them.

2. **Skill level.** Make sure you work with an attorney who specializes in estate planning. You don't want an accident attorney drafting your estate plan. A skilled estate planning attorney will ask for specific details to prepare and file the proper legal documents.

3. **Cost.** The costs to draft your estate plans vary significantly. Some attorneys offer packages and retainers. Getting a one-time planning package works best for most people. But assess which option is best for you.

STEP 3: CHOOSING YOUR MONEY TEAM

You don't have to do this all alone. Regardless of the financial stage you are in, there are professionals who can support you along the way, from money coaches to investment advisors to financial planners to debt counselors. You have options.

I recommend creating a money team to advise and support you. A money team is a group of financial experts with different skills and knowledge. They help you plan for the future, manage your taxes, make smart investments, and protect your assets. Think of them as your financial support crew, helping you make the best decisions for your money.

BUILDING YOUR MONEY TEAM

A money team can consist of different financial experts offering you one-time or continuous guidance.

- **Accountability partner:** Supports you along the way to keep you on track with your goals, usually a friend or someone else sharing similar financial aspirations.

- **Financial planner or CFP®:** Offers comprehensive financial planning, considering various aspects of your life and desired goals.
- **Accountant or CPA:** Provides you with tax planning, prepares tax returns, and ensures you maximize deductions and minimize tax liabilities.
- **Estate planning attorney:** Helps you create wills, trusts, and estate plans to ensure your assets are distributed according to your wishes.
- **Insurance broker:** Assists you in selecting appropriate insurance coverage to protect against risks like health issues, accidents, or unexpected events.

Your money team doesn't have to be limited to these members. Depending on your situation, you can have more or less. Other members include a budget expert, debt coach, financial therapist, business advisor, mortgage broker, real estate agent, investment advisor, and attorney.

We've covered three money team members in this pillar: an accountant, an estate planning attorney, and an insurance professional. It's now time to discuss a key member of your money team: the financial planner.

Working with a Financial Planner

You don't know what you don't know. We all have blind spots. You can benefit from having an expert connect your legacy aspirations with your broader financial plan. Doing so is a way to ensure you're on track. Financial planners provide comprehensive financial planning, help you prioritize goals, and address financial vulnerability.

But the biggest hurdle before choosing a financial planner is overcoming mental and emotional barriers like general anxiety, shame about money, and the fear of being judged. These were the reasons I delayed working with planners. And they might be the reasons why you've avoided working with them too.

Do you need a financial planner right now?

It is possible you don't need one quite yet. This can be the case if you're in extreme credit card debt or living paycheck to paycheck.

Instead, you'd benefit from working with an expert to help balance a budget. There are financial counselors who focus on getting you on a solid financial footing first. You can add one to your money team. For instance, I've collaborated with AFC®s across the country on financial wellness events. An AFC® is a certification held by financial professionals who want to offer comprehensive life-cycle financial education and assist clients in financial decision-making. Many are highly skilled in shifting mindsets, building budgets, and getting out of debt.

I suggest working with a CFP® professional eventually at some point in your journey. They are financial experts who've undergone a rigorous certification training program. A planner with the CFP® designation has formal recognition of expertise and adheres to a set of financial planning practices and principles.

While some people might say you don't need to pay for financial advice, I hold a different opinion. It's helpful to speak to, work with, and get advice from an expert, even if it's just making sure the plan you created yourself has covered all the bases.

Once you decide to add a financial planner to your money team, take your time to find the right person. Don't rush the process. You need to get to know them. You'll work best with some planners. And you may want to avoid others. It's a relationship that must favor your best interest.

You can hire a planner once to create your plan or work with them for years. However, I have learned that working with a financial planner shouldn't be a one-time deal. You'll benefit with a long-term financial relationship. Your life will continue to change, and your plan must change with it. And the more they understand your finances, goals, and lifestyle, the better your financial plan becomes.

HOW TO FIND A FINANCIAL PLANNER

You can start by asking your family and friends. It's also good to ask the other financial professionals you work with for referrals. Consider the following three factors to choose the best planner for your situation.

1. Determine whether or not you need one. If you ask most financial planners, they'll tell you the best time was yesterday.

a. **But do you really need one right now?** The answer depends on your situation, such as your income, profession, and assets. A good rule of thumb is when you start having more questions about your finances.

b. **Are you personally ready to divulge financial information?** You must be willing to share it all so the right plan is created for you.

2. **Understand how advisors are compensated.** There are different fee structures for financial advice, and some can hurt your investment. What are the fee structures?

a. **Fee-only financial advisors are paid for services.** They charge hourly or with a flat rate. For instance, they can charge $250 for a one-hour consultation, offer a monthly service with a fee, or create a plan for a one-time charge. Some fee-only planners might also buy and sell investments for you and charge a percentage of assets under management.

b. **Fee-based financial advisors.** They're like fee-only advisors, except their income can also come from products they've sold to you. They get paid by you and by other sources like commissions from companies.

c. **Commission-based advisors.** They are not paid directly by you and only receive compensation from commissions. It's possible that this type of advisor might only be interested in selling you products without consideration of your situation. That's because the more products they sell, the higher their commissions.

3. **Personality fit.** You have to get along with the planner. Their personality and communication style must meet your needs. And you must trust them to do what's in your best interest and have the expertise to do it well.

a. **Choosing a financial advisor is a big move.** Make sure you do your due diligence. Assess them for their knowledge and fit for your personality. Interview at least three professionals so you can make comparisons.

Finding a CFP® professional

Be mindful that many financial professionals label themselves financial planners. You can mistakenly think they have the CFP® designation. To verify accreditation, check finra.org to review a CFP® professional.

(Continued)

(Continued)

Before committing to a financial planner or CFP®, ask them about their fiduciary responsibilities. A **fiduciary** is bound ethically to act in your best interest and place your benefit above theirs. They must tell you about conflicts of interest that could affect their advice. If a planner refuses to answer the question "Are you a fiduciary?" it's best to walk away and find another.

TAKE ACTION

Use the worksheets found in the Appendix to help you with the action items:

1. Complete the Plan Your Legacy Worksheet.
2. Identify the professionals you need today and start your money team.

Plan Your Legacy Recap

In this chapter, we broke the taboo on money, death, and taxes. You learned that tax strategy is more than just filing returns; it's about protecting your income. You also gained a deeper understanding of estate planning to manage and transfer your assets to loved ones in case of illness and death. And you began the step to build your money team.

The lessons you learned were:

- **Step 1:** Creating your tax strategy
- **Step 2:** Building your estate plan
- **Step 3:** Choosing your money team

Remember, there are things you can do today to protect what you've worked hard to create.

PROTECT MONEY SUMMARY

Congratulations! You did it and finished the fifth pillar. You've mastered making your money smile by protecting what you've worked hard to build.

In the Protect Money pillar, you learned to safeguard your identity and insure your assets. You were introduced to tax strategy and estate planning. You also learned how a money team can help you reach your financial goals, provide peace of mind, and protect your legacy, through these lessons:

- **Lesson 1:** Safeguard Your Identity
- **Lesson 2:** Insure Your Assets
- **Lesson 3:** Plan Your Legacy

And that is it for the pillars! Amazing work!

Conclusion

Woohoo! You've just finished reading through the five Smile Money Pillars.

You are well on your way to money mastery. In the previous chapters, we covered an extensive list of financial matters. Some areas need a deeper dive to grasp fully, but I'm confident you've received the most vital lessons and the simplest steps.

Remember, this book is written to allow you to jump around to the specific pillars you'd like to focus on. I also encourage you to expand on the knowledge you've gained. For additional articles and resources, visit thesmilemoney.com/book

Smile Money Pillars	Summary
Manage	Your **cash flow strategy** directs your money to what's most important.
Earn	Your **income strategy** optimizes your earnings and diversifies your income.
Grow	Your **investing strategy** prioritizes your savings for retirement and independence.
Borrow	Your **credit strategy** shifts your mindset to build wealth using leverage.
Protect	Your **legacy strategy** secures your most valuable assets.

BONUS: SMILE MONEY MILESTONES

The awesomeness of the Smile Money Pillars is that it allows you to jump around and focus on an area that needs more of your attention. But some of you may want more direction. Well, you're in for a treat. Here are my 10 Smile Money Milestones.

Milestones	Pillar
Milestone 1: Have $1,000 in a Rainy Day Fund.	*Manage Money*
Milestone 2: Contributed 10% to 401(k).	*Grow Money*
Milestone 3: Paid off high-interest credit cards.	*Borrow Money*
Milestone 4: Saved into an opportunity fund (six months of living expenses).	*Manage Money*
Milestone 5: Started a side hustle and earned your first $100.	*Earn Money*
Milestone 6: Started investing for independence with $100 per month.	*Earn and Grow Money*
Milestone 7: Contributing the max into your 401(k) plan.	*Grow Money*
Milestone 8: Investing using a Roth IRA (contribute the maximum annual amount).	*Grow Money*
Milestone 9: Funding your cash reserve (12–24 months of living expenses).	*Manage Money*
Milestone 10: Eliminated. all debt.	*Borrow Money*

If you want to determine how you're doing, assess your progress with the first benchmark of each financial goal.

Financial Goals	First Benchmark
Credit card debt balances	$0
First side hustle income	$100
$1k Rainy Day savings	$1,000
401(k) contributions	$10,000
$100k in retirement accounts	$100,000
Financial independence number	$1,000,000

To learn more about the milestones and benchmarks, visit thesmilemoney.com/book.

And feel free to reach out to me directly. You can email me at author@jasonvitug.com. I would love to hear from you. Send me a note and I'll reply with a surprise.

Additional Resources

To learn more about the experts and websites mentioned in this book, please visit thesmilemoney.com/book.

To find the best products and services, visit the financial marketplace at phroogal.com.

For more knowledge and to continue your journey, join the online academy at thesmileuniversity.com.

MY BOOKS

Make Your Money Smile is the third book of the road to financial wellness series. If you haven't read my prior works, check out the summaries below.

You Only Live Once: The Roadmap to Financial Wellness and a Purposeful Life

Time is the most valuable resource you own. Learn how to enjoy today while planning for a better financial tomorrow. *You Only Live Once* redefines the millennial mantra into a practice of mindful financial decision-making to engineer your best life. The financial ACT process in the book will teach you:

- Awareness: Understand your financial starting point and learn to envision your destination.
- Creating a Plan: Build the roadmap to achieve your financial and life goals.
- Taking Control: Learn to spend mindfully, save purposefully, and fix the debt mindset.

Happy Money Happy Life: A Multidimensional Approach to Health, Wealth, and Financial Freedom

You deserve to be happy! In this instant bestseller, Jason shows you how to elevate your relationship with money towards wellness and happiness. Learn to transform your relationship with money into one that powers holistic well-being. In *Happy Money Happy Life*, you'll discover how:

- Happiness is a result of the choices you make and how to improve your money mindset for happier outcomes.
- The overlapping and interconnected nature of your well-being and how to improve every aspect of your eight wellness dimensions: mental, emotional, physical, spiritual, social, occupational, environmental, and financial.
- A nonprescriptive path to financial independence that considers your unique financial challenges, different life stage, and personal goals.

You can learn more about my other works by visiting jasonvitug. com/books.

Appendix

FINANCIAL WELLNESS CHECKUP

What areas need more of your attention? Circle your choice (Yes or No)
and write down any thoughts that come to mind.

Do you feel generally optimistic about your finances? How you're feeling about your situation matters because it affects your health.	Yes / No
Do you know where your money is going? Using a budget or detailed knowledge of how you spend your money is essential.	Yes / No
Do you have an emergency fund? Having money to cover emergencies and unexpected expenses for peace of mind.	Yes / No
Do you have enough for monthly expenses? Your income should cover your needs, wants, and savings goals.	Yes / No
Have you recently paid any service fees? Paying bank fees, late fees, and NSF fees impact your money.	Yes / No
Are you affording monthly debt payments? Debt should be minimized to reduce interest payments and improve cash flow.	Yes / No
Are you contributing to retirement? Take advantage of employer-sponsored plans and IRAs to fund your lifestyle in retirement.	Yes / No
Are you investing for independence? Invest money into a general investing account to regain your time freedom.	Yes / No
Do you have other forms of income? Don't rely solely on a paycheck. Income diversification is essential.	Yes / No
Do you have a healthcare plan? Health issues are the leading cause of financial stress.	Yes / No
Do you have a tax-saving strategy? Optimize your income withholding and reduce your future tax obligations.	Yes / No
Do you have life insurance? Protect your loved ones by giving them a safety net.	Yes / No
Do you have an estate plan? Indicate how you want your assets distributed.	Yes / No

(Continued)

Do you use all or most of your employee benefits? Use your salary and benefits to achieve goals.	Yes / No
Do you work with a money expert or a financial advisor? Get help and find answers to your specific financial situation and challenges.	Yes / No

MANAGE PILLAR

Lesson 1: Elevate Your Banking Relationships

Review Current Banking Relationship

1. Evaluate your existing banking relationships.
2. Decide whether your current financial institution serves your needs.

Account Type	Financial Institution	Primary Account	Monthly Fee	Direct Deposit	Last Used	Comments
Checking (example)	ABC Bank	Yes	$5	Yes, my paycheck	Current	Paid 1 NSF fee in last 6 months
Checking (example)	123 Credit Union	No	$0	No	Not active	Access to surcharge free ATMs, no monthly fees, and no overdraft fees

How to request ChexSystems Report

1. Get your free copy of ChexSystems report by visiting www.ChexSystems.com.

   ▪ You are entitled to a free copy of your ChexSystems consumer report, at your request, once every 12 months.

   ▪ If you were denied a bank account because of information found in your ChexSystems report, then you have the right to request a copy of the report and the opportunity to dispute inaccuracies. Request a copy of your report. Then review the report completely.

Date Requested:		Any Reported Issues?	Yes [ ] No [ ]
Financial Institution	Reported Issue	Comments	Resolution
Reporting company	Adverse Action items (List all adverse action items found in your report.) **What type of issue is reported?**	Contact financial institutions or disputed on ChexSystems?	Has the issue been resolved? (Write down the results.)
ABC Bank (example)	Unpaid nonsufficient funds	Contacted on April 3.	Paid off NSF amount. Adverse item will be removed.

Lesson 2: Create Your Budget

List your income and expenses using the worksheet.

Monthly Income and Expenses List			
Income	Amount	Expenses	Amount
Income Total		Expenses Total	

Complete the Needs and Wants checklist.

What are your financial needs?

Your needs include things that are essential, like shelter. It can also include obligations, like debt, that are required.

✓	Needs Checklist
	Housing: Mortgage or rent
	Homeowner's or renter's insurance
	Property tax (if not already included in the mortgage payment)
	Auto insurance

✓	Needs Checklist
	Health insurance
	Out-of-pocket healthcare costs, copayments, prescriptions
	Utilities: electrical, gas, water
	Internet
	Cell phone
	Life insurance
	Groceries and household goods
	Transportation: car, gas, tolls, public, rideshare
	Debt payments: student loans, installment loans
	Credit card balances: minimum payments
	Other loans: monthly payments
	Child support or alimony payments
	Wellness programs: gym membership
	Care: childcare, adult care, daycare

What are your financial wants?

Your wants are things that are nice to have but aren't necessary. However, they might be essential to improving your quality of life. For instance, it's not necessary to dine at restaurants, but you may want to.

✓	Wants checklist
	Entertainment: movies, events, concerts
	Clothing
	Dining out
	Prepaid meals and food delivery
	Conventions and conferences
	Subscriptions: news, streaming shows, music
	Travel: airline tickets, hotels, rental cars, etc.
	Cable and home phone
	Additional perks: cell phone insurance

Identify at least three financial goals using SMART.

A goal is much easier to reach when it is SMART, meaning it includes the five elements.

SMART Goals	
A goal that is Specific has a much greater chance of being reached.	**Is the goal clearly defined and specific?**
A goal that is **Measurable** means you can track your progress, which helps you stay motivated.	Can progress towards the goal be quantified or measured?
A goal that is **Attainable** is within the realm of possibility based on your skills and resources.	Is the goal realistic and attainable within the given limits?
A goal that is **Relevant** ensures it aligns with your values.	Does the goal align with broader objectives and priorities?
A goal that is **Timely** has a deadline or target date.	What is the deadline or time frame for achieving the goal?

What goal do you want to reach?	
Specific	
Measurable	
Attainable	
Relevant	
Time-bound	

What goal do you want to reach?	
Specific	
Measurable	
Attainable	
Relevant	
Time-bound	

What goal do you want to reach?	
Specific	
Measurable	
Attainable	
Relevant	
Time-bound	

Lesson 3: Cash Flow Your Money

Calculate your monthly cash flow using the Income Worksheet.

Income List	Net Monthly Income Example	Your Net Monthly Income
Salary	$4,300	$
Other Income:_____	$1,000	$
Other Income:_____		$
Other Income:_____		$
Other Income:_____		$
Total Income	**$5,300**	**$**

Calculate your monthly expenses using the BDO Worksheet.

Expense List	Monthly Expense Example	Your Monthly Expense
Bills		
Rent	$1,500	$
Electricity	$200	$
Transportation	$200	$
Groceries	$300	$
Cell service	$75	$
Debt		
Mortgage	$0	$
Car loan	$350	$
Credit card	$100	$
Student loan	$150	$
Optional		
Clothing	$50	$
Entertainment	$50	$
Subscriptions	$50	$
Dining	$100	$

Expense List	Monthly Expense Example	Your Monthly Expense
Savings Goals		
Rainy Day	$25	$
Opportunity Fund	$25	$
Car downpayment	$0	$
Total	**$3,175**	**$**

Calculate your cash flow number

What's your cash flow?

It's now time to put the numbers together. Do the math: subtract your expenses from your income.

$$\textbf{Net Monthly Income (Money In) – Monthly Expenses}$$
$$\textbf{(Money Out) = Cash Flow}$$

	Income (Money In)	Minus	Expenses (Money Out)	Equals	Cash Flow
Cash Flow Example	$5,300	–	$3,175	=	$2,125
Your Cash Flow	$	–	$	=	$

How are you living?

Cash Flow Analysis: How are you living? (circle one)	
Within	You're doing well, but it might lead to future financial trouble if unexpected expenses arise or income is disrupted.
Above	You're living on borrowed money, which means you're experiencing a great deal of financial stress.
Below	You're financially healthy and can treat yourself a bit while contributing more towards your goals.

Complete the Spend Less Matrix

Review the expense list and write down in this matrix the expenses you can eliminate, negotiate, reduce, and consolidate.

Spend Less Matrix	
Eliminate	Negotiate
Reduce	Consolidate

Complete the Spend Less Worksheet

Use this worksheet to help you eliminate, negotiate, consolidate, and reduce your expenses.

1. Use your expenses from your expense lists.
2. Identify the contact info to discuss with your billers.
3. Calculate your savings.
4. Indicate the action and comments for follow-up, if necessary.

Note: It may take you a day to complete the list but will take extra days to contact each provider. Use the list to help you get organized. If you have a hard time eliminating, then try reducing the monthly cost first.

Expenses	Contact Info	Current Bill Amount	Frequency (monthly, quarterly, annually)	New Bill Amount	Savings = Current Bill – New Bill	Action (Eliminate, Negotiate, Consolidate, Reduce)	Comments
Rent (example)	Ms. Cruz ABC Mgmt 888-555-1234	$1800	Monthly	$1700	$100	Negotiate	Spoke with landlord on Feb 1. Lower rent begins next month.
Rent/ Mortgage		$		$	$		
Electricity		$		$	$		
Water		$		$	$		
Gas/Other		$		$	$		
Internet		$		$	$		
Cell Service		$		$	$		
Cable		$		$	$		
Home Phone		$		$	$		
Auto Insurance		$		$	$		
Subscriptions		$		$	$		
		$		$	$		

Expenses	Contact Info	Current Bill Amount	Frequency (monthly, quarterly, annually)	New Bill Amount	Savings = Current Bill – New Bill	Action (Eliminate, Negotiate, Consolidate, Reduce)	Comments
		$		$	$		
		$		$	$		
		$		$	$		
		$		$	$		
		$		$	$		
		$		$	$		
		$		$	$		

Complete Purposeful Savings Plan Worksheet

	Goal	Amount Needed	Monthly Contribution
Rainy Day Fund	$1000	$	$
Happy Fund	1-month salary for wellness, vacation	$	$
Opportunity Fund	6 months of basic living expenses	$	$
Freedom Fund	12 months of living expenses	$	$
Cash Reserve	24 months of living expenses	$	$

What are your other savings goals?

Purposeful Savings	Goal	Amount Needed	Monthly Contribution
		$	$
		$	$
		$	$

Complete the Automation Checklist

Use this worksheet to help you automate your finances.

Automation List	Date Completed
Completed review of primary checking account	
Enrolled in direct deposit	

Automation List	Date Completed
Enrolled in e-statements	
Contributions to employer-sponsored retirement plans set	
Purposeful savings funds: auto-savings transfers set	
Other savings accounts: auto-savings transfers set	
Mortgage or rent: auto-payment set	
Utilities: auto-payments set	
Utilities: auto-payments set	
Cell phone services: auto-payment set	
Credit cards: auto-payments set	
Student loans: auto-payments set	
Other debts: auto-payments set	

EARN PILLAR

Lesson 1: Optimize Your Paycheck

Review Your Paycheck

Let's review your pay stub. This assignment gets you familiar with each section and may lead to asking very important questions.

1. Get your last pay stub.
2. Use this checklist to review each section.
3. Add comments or notes to follow up with your human resources manager.

Pay Stub Review			
	Current Pay Period	Year-to-Date (YTD)	Comments
Gross Earnings	$	$	
FICA Med Tax	$	$	
FICA SS Tax	$	$	
Federal Tax	$	$	
State Tax	$	$	

Pay Stub Review			
	Current Pay Period	Year-to-Date (YTD)	Comments
Pre-tax Contributions			
Retirement	$	$	
Health Insurance	$	$	
Health Savings Account (HSA)	$	$	
Flexible Spending Account	$	$	
Other: _____	$	$	
Other: _____	$	$	
Other: _____	$	$	
After-tax Contributions			
	$	$	
	$	$	
	$	$	
	$	$	
Net Pay Direct Deposited	$	$	

Paycheck Review: Circle yes or no

- Is your personal information correct? Yes / No
- Is your hourly rate or salary reported correctly? Yes / No
- Are your deductions and/or contributions being deducted in the correct amounts? Yes / No
- Do you have the right number of allowances for tax-withholding purposes? Yes / No

What Pre-Tax Contributions Are You Making?

✓	Common Pre-tax Contributions Checklist	
	401(k) Contributions	The money you contribute to a 401(k) retirement plan is deducted before taxes, helping you save for retirement while reducing your taxable income.
	Health Insurance Premiums	If your employer offers health insurance, your premiums are often deducted pre-tax, making it more affordable to maintain coverage.

✓	Common Pre-tax Contributions Checklist	
	Flexible Spending Account (FSA)	Money contributed to an FSA for medical expenses, dependent care, or transportation costs is taken out of your paycheck before taxes.
	Health Savings Account (HSA)	Contributions to an employer's HSA plan are pre-tax. It's used for qualified medical expenses and can be used to cover eligible healthcare costs.
	Transportation Commuter Benefits	If your employer provides commuter benefits for public transportation or qualified parking expenses, the amount is deducted pre-tax.
	Dental and Vision Insurance Premiums	Similar to health insurance, premiums for dental and vision coverage can often be deducted before taxes.
	Group Life Insurance Premiums	If your employer offers group life insurance, the premiums may be deducted pre-tax.
	Qualified Tuition Assistance	Some employers offer tuition assistance or reimbursement programs, and the benefits are typically pre-tax.
	Qualified Adoption Assistance	If you're adopting a child, certain adoption-related expenses can be deducted pre-tax.
	Union Dues	If you're a union member, your dues may be taken from your paycheck before taxes.
	Legal Assistance Plans	Some employers offer pre-tax deductions for legal assistance plans.
	Retirement Savings for Self-Employed	If you're self-employed, contributions to individual retirement accounts (IRAs) can be deducted before taxes.

Maximizing Your Earnings Using Employer Benefits

What benefits and perks are offered and what are you using?

Benefits and Perks	Offered or Using
Paid time off (vacation, sick, other)	
401(k) employer match	
Health insurance (health, dental, vision)	
Health Savings Account / Flexible Spending Account	
Group term life insurance	
Disability insurance	

Benefits and Perks	Offered or Using
Stocks (options, restricted units)	
Employee stock purchase program	
Tuition reimbursement	
Public transportation credit	
Student loan payment program	
Wellness programs (gym, healthy habits, workshops)	
Childcare	
In-office perks (snacks, lunches)	
Telecommuting / Flexible work schedule	
Employee Assistance Program	
Credit union	
Discounts (shopping portals, affinity discounts)	

Access Your Social Security Statement

What's your current lifetime earnings?

The Social Security Statement shows your record of all earnings received during your work history. The SSA keeps it to determine your eligibility for Social Security benefits upon retirement or disability.

1. Access your Social Security Statements online through SSA.gov.

	Amount	Years	Example
Social Security Statement Reported Total Earnings	$		What are your earning years? Ex. 2003 – 2018 = 15 years
Average Yearly Earnings	$	X	What are your average yearly earnings? Ex. $875,450 total earnings / 15 years = $58,363

Get Your Pay Raise Checklist

After reading the section on getting a pay raise, use the questionnaire to guide you.

Pay Raise Questions to Prepare Yourself	
Step 1: Answer the questions.	Do you really deserve a pay raise? Yes / No Why do you deserve a raise? Answer with a list of accomplishments that first come to mind.
Step 2: Read your current job description.	Request the job description from your HR manager.
Step 3: Get reliable market data.	Visit salary.com to start your research.
Step 4: List all your significant accomplishments.	Create a spreadsheet to list your accomplishments. Be specific. Include the date, accomplishment/recognition, managers involved, and any recommendations. For example, you saved your department X dollars, introduced a new process, received a reward, got a new certification, etc. Have you added significant accomplishments and certifications to your resume? Yes / No
Step 5: Choose the right time.	Schedule a time to speak with your manager when it's best for them and you. Are you having workplace performance issues? Yes / No Are there major project deadlines in the calendar? Yes / No
Step 6: Know the financials of your company.	Is it profitable or in the red? Yes / No Is your department achieving its goals? Yes/ No

Increasing Your Salary	
Have you updated your resume?	**Yes / No**
Have you updated your LinkedIn profile?	Yes / No
Have you scheduled time with your manager?	Yes / No First date: _____

Work Accomplishments and Commendations List

1. Use this as a template to create your spreadsheet. Examples are given.
2. List all your accomplishment as they happen. Add certifications, awards, and recommendations from others.
3. Remember to update your resume and LinkedIn with only the significant accomplishments.

Accomplishment or Commendation	Date	Manager/ Coworker	Comments
Reduced department expenses by 10%	October 2021	Sam Perez	Part of a team that worked with leadership and the finance department to reduce overhead.
Service award	December 2021	CEO	Got company recognition for my commitment to the company.

Lesson 2: Multiply Your Income Streams

What's Your Income Number?

List all your income streams in the table and indicate what type they are.

Income Number			
Income	Gross Monthly Amount	Gross Annual Amount	Type (active, passive, portfolio)
	$	$	
	$	$	

Income Number		
	$	$	
	$	$	
	$	$	
	$	$	
Total	**$**	**$**	
Income Number (Total of Income Types)		

What's Your Side Hustle?

Answer these questions to get your ideas flowing.

Side hustle idea questions	Ideas
What stuff can you sell?	
What service can you offer?	
Do you have a driver's license and a car?	
Do you have unused space and enjoy hosting?	
Are you a skilled wordsmith, artist, photographer, or graphic designer?	

Lesson 3: Diversify Your Income Sources

How Many Income Sources Do You Currently Have?

Complete this checkup.

Income Sources Checkup		
Sources	**Description**	**Do you have any?**
Earned Income	Money earned from exchanging your time	Yes / No
Profit Income	Money earned from business profits	Yes / No
Rental Income	Money earned from rental properties	Yes / No
Royalty Income	Money earned from licensing creations	Yes / No
Interest Income	Money earned from lending to others	Yes / No
Dividend Income	Money earned from stocks and funds	Yes / No
Capital Gains	Money earned from selling assets	Yes / No

Complete the Worksheet by Listing Your Income

Identify the types of income you currently have and the ones you desire to create.

Income Strategy Worksheet			
Income List	Source *(active, passive, portfolio)*	Stream Type *(earned, rental, profit, royalty, interest, dividend, capital gains)*	Existing or Planned *Income is current or planned for future*

GROW PILLAR

Lesson 1: Build Your Investments

Checkup: How are you investing?			
Do you have. . .	Amount Invested	Current Annual Contribution	Contributing for employer match
Savings account	$	$	—
Retirement plan 401(k), 403(b), 457(b)	$	$	Yes / No
IRA Traditional or Roth	$	$	—
General investing Taxable brokerage account	$	$	—

Calculate how long it will take for your savings to double using the Rule of 72.

RULE OF 72: WHEN WILL YOUR MONEY DOUBLE?

The rule of 72 is a simple mathematical shortcut to estimate the time it takes for money to double in value at a given interest rate.

To use the rule of 72, divide the number 72 by the interest rate. The answer is the number of years it will take for your money to double.

72 / Annual Rate of Return = Number of Years for Amount to Double

For example, if you save money at a 6% interest rate, it will take about 12 years to double.

72	Divided	Annual Rate	Equals	Years
72	÷	6	=	12

The rule of 72 is a simple way to get a rough estimate, but it's not always accurate. The actual number of years it takes for money to double will depend on the exact interest rate, the consistency of that rate, and other factors, such as compounding.

Give it a try: How long will it take for your money to double? Check the current interest rate you're earning on a savings account.

72	Divided	Annual Rate	Equals	Years
72	÷		=	

CD Ladder Strategy

Use this table to create your own CD Ladder Strategy

Account Type	Interest	Amount	Maturity
Savings account		$	
30-day CD		$	
3-month CD		$	
6-month CD		$	
9-month CD		$	
12-month CD		$	
15-month CD		$	
18-month CD		$	
Total		$	

The CDs roll over into a new term if the money is not withdrawn. For instance, if your 6-month CD matures and you do nothing, it'll renew into another 6-month CD with the current interest rate.

Lesson 2: Contribute to Your Retirement

Estimate Your Retirement Goal Using the Rule of 25

The rule of 25 is a helpful way to determine how much money you'll need at retirement.

Use the following equation:

Retirement Goal = Annual Lifestyle Expense × 25

With a $50,000 projected lifestyle expense, you'll need about $1,250,000 saved.

Projected Annual Lifestyle Expense	Multiply by 25	Retirement Goal
$50,000	x 25	$1,250,000

Now, it's your turn: Calculate your projected lifestyle expense in retirement to determine your retirement goal.

Projected Annual Lifestyle Expense	Multiply by 25	Retirement Goal
$	x 25	$

If your retirement goal seems inflated because of your current lifestyle, reimagine the lifestyle of your dreams. You have control over your future lifestyle expenses.

Lesson 3: Invest for Independence

How to Calculate Your FI Number

Here's the first part: To get your FI number, you'll need your monthly expenses multiplied by 12 (months). As an example, let's use $3,333 as a monthly expense.

Monthly Expenses × 12 = Total Yearly Expenses

Monthly Expenses	Multiply	12 Months	Equals	Total Yearly Expenses
$3,333	x	12	=	$40,000

Now it's your turn: Calculate your total yearly expenses.

Monthly Expenses	Multiply	12 Months	Equals	Total Yearly Expenses
$	x	12	=	$

Here's the second part: Use the rule of 25. Look at your total yearly expenses and multiply that by 25.

Financial Independence Number = Yearly Expenses × 25

For example, if your total yearly expenses equal to $40,000, you'll need $1,000,000 ($40,000 × 25) saved.

Give it a try: How much do you need saved? What is your FI number?

Yearly Expenses	Multiply	25	Equals	FI Number
$40,000	x	25	=	$1,000,000
$	x	25	=	$

Remember, the lower your monthly expenses, the lower your FI number can be.

How Much Can You Withdraw?

For instance, your $1,000,000 investment allows you to withdraw $40,000 annually and indefinitely when using the 4% rule or safe withdrawal rate (SWR).

Investment Portfolio	Multiply	4%	Equals	Safe Withdrawal Amount
$1,000,000	x	0.04 or 4%	=	$40,000

Now, it's your turn: Calculate how much you can safely withdraw. Use the FI number you calculated earlier.

Investment Portfolio	Multiply	4%	Equals	Safe Withdrawal Amount
$	x	0.04 or 4%	=	$

(Continued)

(*Continued*)

Now, once your **Investment Portfolio** reaches your **FI Number**, you're able to live off your investments and can **safely withdraw** money to pay for **Yearly Expenses**.

How Long Will It Take to Reach Financial Independence?

If you enjoy calculations, use the following equation to estimate the time it'll take to reach FI:

Years to FI = (FI Number − Existing Portfolio Amount) / Yearly Savings

- **Existing Portfolio Amount:** The total amount of money already saved that includes retirement accounts, investable accounts (brokerage, stocks, etc.), pensions, and other savings accounts.
- **Yearly Savings:** The amount of money you invest monthly multiplied by 12 months.

For example, let's say your FI number is $1,000,000, and you already have $250,000 in existing investment portfolios. You would need to save $750,000 more to reach your number. Assuming you can save $25,000 annually, it would take you 30 years.

Your calculation would look like this: ($1,000,000 − $250,000) / $25,000 = 30 Years to FI

FI Number	Minus	Existing Portfolio Amount	Divided	Yearly Savings	Equals	Years to FI
$1,000,000	−	$250,000	÷	$25,000	=	30

This calculation is helpful but it's a simple one. It does not take into account the compound growth of investments. If your investments have an average 7% rate of return per year, you will reach FI in 12 years, not 30. That is the power of investing.

Now, it's your turn: How many years will it take to reach your FI number? Use the calculation to estimate.

FI Number	Minus	Existing Portfolio Amount	Divided	Yearly Savings	Equals	Years to FI
$	−	$	÷	$	=	

Next, try an online calculator using a 7% rate of return. Go to thesmilemoney.com/book.

Online Calculator Estimate (Years to FI)	$

Compare the two. You'll notice the power of compounding and how that can take years off the path to financial independence.

Keep this in mind: You can reduce the Years to FI by increasing your monthly investing amount or earning a higher rate of return.

How Do You Select the Right Brokerage Service?

Ask yourself the following questions:

- Do I prefer a hands-on approach or a more automated, hands-off approach?
- How comfortable am I with managing my investments independently?
- Am I confident in making buy and sell decisions on my own?
- Do I have the time and interest to research and monitor investments regularly?
- How important is personalized guidance and advice in managing my investments?
- Am I looking for a cost-effective solution to execute trades, or am I willing to pay higher fees for additional services?
- Do I have complex financial needs like tax planning, estate planning, or risk management?
- What is my risk tolerance? Am I comfortable with potential fluctuations in the value of my investments?
- Do I have a specific retirement goal or other financial milestones I want to achieve?

Based on your answers, determine which aligns with your needs.

- If you **prefer more control** over your investments and have the time and knowledge to manage them independently, an online brokerage is the best choice.
- If you **want automated investment management** and guided advice based on your goals and risk tolerance, a robo-advisor could be suitable.
- If you **have complex financial needs**, a significant amount of assets, and desire personalized financial planning, a wealth management service may be the right option.

BORROW PILLAR

Lesson 2: Enhance Your Credit Report and Credit Score

Request Your Free Credit Report

Three major credit bureaus:

Credit Bureau	Website	Telephone
Experian	www.experian.com	(888) 397-3742
TransUnion	www.transunion.com	(800) 916-8800
Equifax	www.equifax.com	(866) 349-5191

To comply with the FCRA, the three major credit bureaus have set up one website, a toll-free telephone number, and a mailing address through which you can order your free annual report.

Choose one of the following to order your free copy:

- Visit AnnualCreditReport.com (the quickest way)
- Call 1-877-322-8228
- Complete an Annual Credit Report Request Form and mail it to:

Annual Credit Report Request Service
P.O. Box 105281
Atlanta, GA 30348-5281

Verify Your Credit Report

Review the sections and look for inaccuracies in personal information, accounts, payment history, and any unfamiliar or suspicious entries.

Credit Report Verification Checklist		
Credit Report Section	Description	Notes
Personal information	Verify your name, Social Security, date of birth, current and previous addresses, and phone numbers.	
Employer information	Verify current and previous employers.	
Credit accounts	Verify account status (closed, opened), creditor names, date opened, credit limits, balances, and payment history.	
Inquiries	View soft and hard inquiries. Verify hard inquiries are from your attempts to acquire credit.	
Collection items	Verify for any outstanding collection reported.	
Public records	Verify accuracy of public records such as bankruptcy, civil suits, foreclosures, judgments, or liens.	

Review each report from the major credit bureaus. Check after completion.	Experian [ ] TransUnion [ ] Equifax [ ]

Credit Accounts Discrepancy Worksheet

Create a list of all the errors you've identified. Include the specific item in question, and a brief explanation of why you believe it's inaccurate.

Credit Bureau (which report did you review?): Experian [ ] TransUnion [ ] Equifax [ ]			
Account in Question	Creditor or Furnisher	Issue	Comments

Credit Bureau (which report did you review?): Experian [ ] TransUnion [ ] Equifax [ ]			
Account in Question	Creditor or Furnisher	Issue	Comments

Credit Bureau (which report did you review?): Experian [ ] TransUnion [ ] Equifax [ ]			
Account in Question	Creditor or Furnisher	Issue	Comments

Get Your Credit Score

Request free credit scores from the companies listed in the chart.

Source	Credit Score	Credit Bureau (Experian, TransUnion, Equifax)	Scoring Method (FICO®, VantageScore, other)
Experian. com (example)	748	Experian	FICO®
Experian.com			
Credit Karma			
Credit Wise			
Other:			
Other:			

Calculate Your Credit Utilization

Review your credit report for open credit cards, including your personal and home lines of credit. Add your credit balances together and do the same for credit limits.

Credit Cards and Lines of Credit	Credit Limit	Current Balance	Comments
	$	$	
	$	$	
	$	$	
	$	$	
	$	$	
	$	$	
	$	$	
	$	$	
	$	$	
	$	$	
	$	$	
	$	$	
	$	$	
Total	$	$	

Then use the calculation in the next chart.

Combined Current Balances	Divided By	Total Credit Limit	Multiply By	100	Equals	Credit Utilization %
$	÷	$	X	100	=	

Lesson 3: Eliminate Your Debt

Debt Prioritization Worksheet

Identify your debt by listing the relevant items in the worksheet. Do the following:

- **Compile your debts:** Make a list of all your debts, including credit card balances, loans, mortgages, medical bills, and any other outstanding obligations. Include the names of creditors, outstanding balances, interest rates, and minimum monthly payments.

- **Calculate total debt:** Add up the total amount you owe across all debts. This gives you a comprehensive view of your overall debt load.

- **Use the worksheet to prioritize debt repayment.** Determine if you'll use the avalanche or the snowball method.

Debt Type (mortgage, credit card, car loan, line of credit, etc.)	Creditor	Outstanding Balance (use for debt snowball)	Interest Rate (use for debt avalanche)	Minimum Monthly Payment	Current Status (on-time, late, unpaid)	Comments
		$		$		
		$		$		
		$		$		
		$		$		
		$		$		
		$		$		
		$		$		
		$		$		
		$		$		
		$		$		
		$		$		
		$		$		
		$		$		
	Total	$	Total	$	—	—

Protect Pillar

Secure Your Personal Information Checklist

Use this checklist to secure your information.

✓	Secure Your Personal Information Checklist	
	Set up account alerts.	Many creditors, banks, and credit unions offer alerts to notify you of transactions ranging from deposits to withdrawals to purchases and payments. You can quickly spot issues before they become major problems.
	Limit sharing your Social Security number.	Don't share your number with anyone who isn't authorized. Always ask why your social security is required.
	Shred your statements.	Dispose of financial statements, credit card statements, pay stubs, and bank records properly. Blackout any identifying information such as your name, address, and account numbers. If possible, shred the documents.
	Use credit cards for purchases.	With credit cards, you get more legal protection compared to debit cards. In the event of fraud, you're not out of money in your checking account. Many card companies offer zero liability and an easy dispute process.
	Enroll your numbers on the Do Not Call registry. Visit donotcall.gov.	Limit the number of companies calling you. The National Do Not Call Registry is a government registry that allows you to enter your home and cell phone numbers to prevent telemarketing calls.
	Monitor your credit report regularly.	Consider using a credit monitoring service that tracks the information found in your report and sends alerts and notifications of changes. There are free and paid services available.
	Enroll in an identity theft protection service and insurance.	These paid services monitor your email and Social Security number on the dark web. They notify you when your personal info appears on these sites. They also provide fraud resolution support and insurance for covered losses.

Keep Your Data Safe Checklist

Complete this checklist to help keep your data safe.

✓	Keeping Your Data Safe Checklist	
	Review financial and billing statements.	Look closely for charges you did not make. Even a small charge can be a warning sign. Thieves sometimes will make a small debit against your checking account and charge more if the small amount goes unnoticed.
	Request credit reports.	Get a copy of your free credit reports from AnnualCreditReport.com. Review the details (refer back to the Borrow Money pillar). Look for names, addresses, and accounts you don't recognize.
	Don't ignore bills from any creditors.	A mysterious billing statement may be an indication that someone else has opened an account in your name. Contact the creditor immediately.
	Protect your PINs and other passwords.	Avoid using easily available information such as your mother's maiden name, birth date, the last four digits of your Social Security number, and phone number. Identity thieves can use this information to access your accounts.
	Use multiple email accounts.	Use different emails for personal use, social media, financial accounts, and subscription services. You may also have separate emails for newsletters and marketing offers.
	Use different passwords.	Have different passwords to prevent scammers from hacking into other accounts. Using a password management service can be useful.
	Place a security freeze.	If you're not looking at applying or opening new credit accounts, consider placing a security freeze on your credit profiles. It prevents new creditors from accessing your credit file.
	Remove your name from marketing offers. Visit optoutprescreen.com.	Opting out prevents consumer credit reporting agencies from providing your credit file information to marketers for prescreened offers.

Are Your Deposits Insured?

Determine if your deposits are covered; speak with someone at your financial institution. Use the table provided.

Financial Institution	Contact	Verified Coverage	Comments
ABC Bank	800-123-4567	Yes, fully insured	

Disability Insurance Checkup

Speak with your HR manager to learn about your disability insurance benefit. Use this table and check the boxes once completed.

Disability Insurance Checkup		✓
Company	Verified disability insurance benefits with HR. How much are you covered? _____	
Personal (optional)	Researched individual disability insurance plans.	

Protecting Your Stuff

Review your auto, homeowner's, or renter's insurance to verify how much of your personal stuff is covered. Determine if your assets are covered in the event of damage or loss. Use the table provided.

Insurance Type	Insurance Company	Coverage Amount
Auto	Gecko	Comprehensive coverage up to the market value of the car for total loss.
Home		
Auto		
Renter's		
Other:		

Assets and Liabilities

Calculate your net worth by listing your assets and liabilities.

Net Worth			
Assets	**Value of Assets**	**Liabilities**	**Outstanding Balances**
	$		$
	$		$
	$		$
	$		$
	$		$
	$		$
	$		$
	$		$
	$		$
Value of Assets Total	$	**Outstanding Balances Total**	$

Net worth = Assets (what you own) – Liabilities (what you owe)

Assets (what you own)	Minus	Liabilities (what you owe)	Equals	Net Worth
$	–	$	=	$

Protect Money Checklist

Use this table to indicate if you have or will do the following:

✓	Protect Your Money	Comments
	Using a credit report monitoring app	
	Have identity theft insurance	
	Reviewed homeowners or renter's insurance	
	Have life insurance (term, whole, or group)	
	Have disability insurance	

✓	Protect Your Money	Comments
	Have long-term care insurance	
	Have a tax strategy	
	Reviewed W4 withholding	
	Spoke with an advisor about estate planning	
	Have a last will and testament	
	Have a trust	
	Have a financial power of attorney	
	Have a healthcare power of attorney	
	Have a living will	
	Reviewed joint accounts or titles (Rights of Survivorship)	
	Added beneficiaries: all banking accounts	
	Added beneficiaries: insurance policies	
	Added beneficiaries: brokerage accounts	
	Added beneficiaries: retirement plans	
	Added beneficiaries: annuity plans	
	Listed all digital assets	
	Designate access to legacy social media	

Acknowledgments

This book would not have been possible without you, my readers, who have supported my writing for years. I appreciate each and every one of you.

To my loving family, who continue to support my wildest dreams and my creative efforts. Thank you to my parents, my siblings and in-laws, my nieces and nephews, aunts and uncles, and cousins. And to my special pup, Shund, who loves to lie next to me as I write, and reminds me it's time to get up and move.

I'm so grateful for my friends, who continue to cheer me on and have been with me through all the ups and downs, the twists and turns, and remain solidly in my corner. You are all very special to me. And to my new friends I met during my book tour, we've forged a life-long connection.

To all the experts mentioned in this book, thank you for sharing your wisdom and helping make this book impactful. I also want to thank the team at Wiley—Susan Cerra, Jean-Karl Martin, and Matt Adamson—for their continued support, especially my editor, Kevin Harreld, who believes I have so much more to share with the world.

These acknowledgments wouldn't be complete without naming the many people who continue to open doors to spread my message of health, wealth, and happiness. Thank you to Bo McDonald, Frank Allgood, and the team behind Your Marketing Co.; David Snodgrass, Linda Douglas, and Megan Green at Lake Trust Credit Union; Leslie Ramsdell and Katie Mills at Sierra Pacific Credit Union; Beth Hottel and Keith Robbennolt at Sentinel Federal Credit Union; Mark Cochran and Robin Lorenzen at Jeanne D'Arc Credit Union; BJ Fillingame at Lookout Credit Union; Grant Gallagher at Affinity Federal Credit Union; Whitney Townsend and Susan Johnson at Fort Community Credit Union; Jennifer Graves and Ryan Roberts at Great Meadow Federal Credit Union; Denise Deem and Tyler Valentine at StagePoint Federal Credit Union; and Gigi Hyland at the National Credit Union

Foundation. Your commitment to financial well-being inspires me and I'm grateful you've allowed me to share the message with your staff and community. I look forward to continuing to work together.

And to some special friends: Miranda Marquit, for spending time to share the beauty that is Idaho; Michael Murdoch, who continues to champion credit union values; Nicole DiDomenico, for hosting me at Norwich University; Adam Grover, who believes deeply in my mission and driving three hours to support an event; Lauren Cobello of Leverage with Media, who gave me confidence to go on live television.

To all my creator friends, podcasters, bloggers, and YouTubers who opened their communities and allowed me to share my message, thank you. Let's continue to make an impact.

And to all the independent bookstores—16 in total—that carried my books and worked with me during my tours. I am grateful for your support and it was a pleasure supporting your bookstore. I hold firmly in my belief that you provide an essential service and space for people and communities.

I'm sure I'm missing many others who helped make this book a reality. Just know I hold you dear in my heart and you're forever part of my journey.

About the Author

Jason Vitug is a wellness expert, a world traveler, and an award-winning writer and *New York Times*–reviewed author of two bestsellers, *You Only Live Once: The Roadmap to Financial Wellness and a Purposeful Life* and *Happy Money Happy Life: A Multidimensional Approach to Health, Wealth, and Financial Freedom*.

Jason left his successful corporate career to pursue a more fulfilling life, which led him on a backpacking journey around the world to discover the true meaning of happiness and success. He continues to travel and experience the world, turning moments into memories and sharing his adventures through his stories. He has traveled to 49 states and visited more than 40 countries. He's one of 5 kids and uncle to 12 nieces and nephews. He's also a super-proud dog dad.

Jason holds a bachelor's in finance from Rutgers University and a Norwich University MBA. He's a certified diversity, equity, and inclusion expert, holds the Psychology of Financial Planning certification, and is also a certified yoga teacher and breathwork specialist.

In his free time, you can find him following his curiosities, dabbling with film projects, and enjoying conversations.

You can connect with Jason through his website, jasonvitug.com.

Index